START WITH YES

START WITH YES

DISCOVER THE SPIRITUAL ROOTS TO SUSTAIN YOUR CALLING

LEXI NORELL

Paperback ISBN: 979-8-9898664-8-9
eBook ISBN: 979-8-9898664-9-6
Library of Congress Control Number: 2024927078

Cover and book design by Allison East & North Parade Press
Printed in the United States of America

To my girls, Cora, Ruby, and Emma.
May you say yes to Jesus all the days of your life.
I love you so much.

TABLE OF CONTENTS

INTRODUCTION: WHAT'S YOUR THING?......................9

PART 1: PATH....................................... 13
Chapter 1: A Better Way................................ 15
Chapter 2: A Permanent Spiritual Address 25
Chapter 3: Everyday Obedience.......................... 39
Chapter 4: The Lies of Spiritual Real Estate............... 55

PART 2: POSTURE 65
Chapter 5: Start with Yes 67
Chapter 6: Walk with a Limp............................ 79
Chapter 7: Your Kingdom Calling 89
Chapter 8: Character over Charisma 99
Chapter 9: The Peace of Saying No 111

PART 3: PACE..................................... 123
Chapter 10: Spiritual Grit 125
Chapter 11: Camping 135
Chapter 12: Waiting Well................................ 147
Chapter 13: Real Rest 157

PART 4: PROVISION 169
Chapter 14: Grace Alone 171
Chapter 15: Made for Relationship...................... 183
Chapter 16: God of Resources 191
Chapter 17: One Simple, Brave Yes at a Time 203

What's Your Thing?

Hey there, friend! At this point in my life, there is one thing I know to be certain amongst the ever-growing pile of uncertainties: you and I can have deep and meaningful influence not only on the people around our table but far and wide, and to generations after us. I'm sure of this. Each one of us has a part to play in God's plans and purposes for this world and His people. And spoiler, His plans are just as much for our flourishing as they are to bless and impact others. This is God's way. He invites us to the inner work of obedience and relationship with Him that sets us upright and grounded in His faithfulness and goodness.

The world does not need us "put together and polished" but it does need our surrendered obedience to Jesus. If we wait to be "our best selves" to pursue the calling God has given us, we will never start. God is inviting you to rise up and do the thing set before you, just as you are—the whole of you, at any stage of life. You don't need to get ready to say yes.

One question I love asking people is: "So, what's your thing?" By this I mean, what keeps you up at night? What dreams and passions are you playing out in the shower (don't act like you haven't done this)? What ideas are you jotting down on napkins? What burdens do you carry and feel called to meet with solutions and serving hands? Who are the faces of the people you feel called to, what stage of life are they in, and what are their challenges? These questions hold the stuff of life and the ins and outs of what makes us tick.

While this book holds lots of space for asking questions—What is my purpose? What is my next step of obedience?—it is even more so a book that explores the *how*. How do I go about bringing this God-dream to life? How on earth am I meant to nurture and care for it? How do I get this fire in my belly out in the actual real-life world where it can take on a lifeforce of its own? How do I get from where I'm standing to where I'm going?

There was a time in my life when I was reaching out to all the wrong influences to tell me how to go about bringing my God-dream to fruition. I needed a roadmap with the steps to see my dream manifest, not one that led me to a place of hating the calling and burning out before I could even truly begin. I looked to all kinds of self-help resources from people who made big ol' promises but led to lots of disappointment.

I turned back to pursuing God's way, the ancient rhythms and teachings that God so graciously gives us in His Holy Word. He shows us the path of grace, peace, joy, and faithful obedience, which leads to purpose and a fulfilling life. He put that dream in your heart, and He has already mapped out the path for you to follow to see that dream flourish. It's all there for us. But unlike so many ways that the world offers, His way requires that we become fully committed followers to Him, going back to the foundational roots of abiding in Him, denying self, and walking in obedience. It's only from this place will we find the true and irreplaceable path laid out by the King of Kings Himself for us.

My hope is that you will leave our time together with more spiritual tools in your belt and a clear path forward in pursuing this dream inside you. I can promise you, when we say yes to Jesus we will surely see the seed of our dreams begin to bloom and the roots of those dreams grow deep and strong, immovable and sturdy for the long run.

Thank you for trusting me with your time and your precious dreams. I want to see you fulfill their highest potential for the glory of God, for the good work to be done in you, and for the benefit of others. Let's take this path together, locking arms, pushing forward, probably stumbling more times than not, but at least falling in the right direction. One small but brave yes at a time.

LOVE,

Lexi

PART 1: PATH

ALLOWING GOD

TO DIRECT

OUR PURPOSE

A Better Way

I'm done."

I let the words slip out of my mouth as I sat on the floor leaning against the laundry machine. My crying was muffled by the sound of the laundry swishing and swooshing, and I knew I had a few minutes before my kids would find me. I was full of disappointment: I thought I would be further along in my pursuit of writing and teaching in Christian spaces by now, but I was left exhausted by all the work and grind I had put into making my dreams a reality. And I was worn out by the emotional and physical work of parenting young kids. On top of that I felt guilty: guilty for all the time and mental and emotional energy I had given to the dream of being a Christian author and not given to my family, only to be left with burnout and nothing to show for it. Sitting by the washing machine that day, I whispered, "There has to be a better way. Lord, show me a better way."

Up until that moment on the laundry room floor, I was knee-deep in every self-help book on the market. I loved absorbing their five steps to achieving success, seven practices to unlocking your full potential, or whatever secret sauce to becoming the best version of yourself. I ate it up. Like a drug, I was completely addicted to the grind. I wanted to serve the Lord with my gifts, and I knew He wanted me to write. The books and podcasts that gave me the foolproof steps to greatness fed my desire to be in control. It was all up to me: *my* power, *my* strength, *my* hustle. I was drawn to that. And it worked—until it didn't. I had all these methods and strategies I was trying to achieve, but they were getting me nowhere. Actually, that's a lie; they were getting me somewhere, like to bed late, to unhealthy places of distraction, to heated arguments with my husband, and into easily angered moments with my kids.

My marriage was suffering from the amount of time and energy I was giving to scrolling on my phone and feeding the machine of jealousy and not-enoughness when I saw people achieving my dreams. I wasn't present with my kids. I was consumed with the feeling that I needed to be giving all my attention to my dreams if I wanted to become anyone to someone. On top of that, I developed an anxiety-induced eye twitch; it was adorable. I was in deep emotional distress, starved spiritually, and suffering physically. I thought, *If this is the way to achieve the things God placed in my heart, is this really worth the cost?* I was exasperated and in need of a spiritual (and maybe physical) Ambien.

I finally decided I couldn't sacrifice my life on the altar of achievement. There had to be a better way to do this, but I couldn't see it. God wouldn't give me a dream just to watch me be chewed up and spat out by it, right?

When you reach the end of yourself, you typically have two options. Option one, throw in the dream towel and pick up a lesser ambition like becoming a "PPPMWACBC," a *professional period piece movie watcher and cheese board connoisseur.* Or option two, pull up your big girl sweatpants and find a better way. I wasn't quite ready to go pro with watching period pieces, so I reassessed how I was looking at and engaging with my God-given dreams. I went back to the basics—the simple and unsaturated teachings of Jesus. My mind knew them, but my heart wasn't practicing them.

I uprooted the old soil and began to lay a new foundation. My new groundwork was built on three things: the call to deny myself, to fiercely abide in Jesus, and to walk in a posture of surrendered obedience to His will. You would have thought I was detoxing from hard drugs. Doing life this way was messy, challenging, and uncomfortable. Practicing denying myself, abiding in Jesus, and walking in obedience meant letting go of the control I thought I had over my life. Without control, it felt like I was most definitely backtracking instead of progressing in my dreams.

To my surprise and relief, in a matter of time (far from over night), I began to bear the good fruit of peace, joy, and rest. Externally nothing changed, unless you count my stress acne clearing up as well as that darn eye twitch vanishing, but my soul and mind underwent a whole transformation. Striving? Gone. Needing to hustle and work like time was running out? Kicked out the door. Looking around and comparing myself to others' pace and path? *Hasta la vista*. My assignment to write had a newborn joy and passion within it, and it came without the need to seek validation, comparison, or compromise. I re-learned the biblical ways of walking in obedience and saying yes to assignments God had for me, relying on His ability, faithfulness, and limitlessness to see the calling over my life flourish.

Living the Jesus way at the Jesus pace was almost as uncomfortable as wearing skinny jeans in the rain. Most days I wanted to go back to my own way, but when I did, I was quickly reminded of the burden my own path carried. Creating your own path to fulfill your God-given purpose will only lead you to burnout. God's path to your purpose is probably less sexy than you would imagine for yourself but it's undoubtedly more fulfilling and restorative. Let me tell you, when the fruit of discipleship began to grow in my life, the hard start was worth it.

Trying to Force a Dream

Many of us are carrying God-given dreams in our hearts, and if we take our eyes off of Jesus we often begin killing ourselves striving to manifest those dreams into reality. More times than we're willing to admit, we try our way over choosing the Jesus way. I went full steam ahead and ended up with boob sweat and burnout. And I see countless women doing the same thing when it comes to the important work they have been destined for. I see it every time I get on social media, over coffee with friends, and in countless books I read.

We are overwhelmed with feeling like we should be further along than we are, crippled by the fear that we missed our chance, our one shot at getting it right. And to top it off, we sacrifice so much of our time, emotions, and thoughts toward forcing our dreams prematurely into the world that we end up missing out on the fullness that our real life already holds. We think that "thing" will be a quick fix to all our reasons for being unhappy and unfulfilled.

Everywhere, I see women who are on fire for God, full of passion but tired and disappointed. Look close enough, and behind every successful Christian woman out there doing her thing are thousands who are gutted that they aren't her. Our world has created, celebrated, and nurtured the Christian celebrity, prizing this position above all else. Discipleship is competing in the same arena with social media growth, algorithms, and engagement. Ministry looks a lot more like filters and inspirational graphics, and less and less like eating meals together and showing up on ground zero with our friends and community that need us most.

Have you felt it? The ever-increasing pressure that if you want to build a ministry or "do a thing" for God, you have to become someone else to make it happen. Someone more likable, someone with less mess, someone with endless confidence and charisma. But hold up, honey, that's not all; the numbers next to your social media handle determine whether or not you have made it or will make it. Without followers, you aren't an influencer. And if you're not an influencer, then there isn't a place for you at the table. We are fooled into believing that a better version of who we are already took that seat at the table, like we are all players in some strange spiritual game of musical chairs. This crushing pressure to promote our personal brand, to be like "her," is suffocating the creativity, passion, and giftings God has given countless women.

This climate makes us look in the mirror and question our worth, our voice, and our place. We walk around in search of adoration and approval from total strangers to affirm that we belong. Instead of seeking the approval of God, we seek the approval from the masses. Feeling unstable in our grounding we ask questions like, *Do they like me? Am I enough? Am I too much? Am I doing this right? How can I get them to like me more? Should I start a blog?* So many of us, including myself, have spent countless, and I mean *countless,* hours hustling our mental health and physical health into the ground for the sake of popularity and approval, because at the core, we believe we are worthy if they say we are, and we will be successful if they like us enough. In an approval dependent culture, we don't see another way.

One of the bajillion lies our culture has convinced us to believe is that we must elevate ourselves to do any kind of worthy work. To reach our best selves and our highest potential, we must first and foremost have the prerequisite of a large audience, and said large audience will determine if what we have to say matters. As if that's not enough, we also have been persuaded to believe that only what is done in public places or platforms holds significance, and what we do in private means little to nothing.

I call these lies an enormous pile of garbage.

There's a better way.

I have deep compassion for women who are hesitant to give their yes to Jesus. If you're that person, striving and tired, I want to see you step into the glorious things God has for your life—but without the striving. Not by sucking it up and working harder, or mustering up more willpower, but by simple obedience, relying solely on our sustainable, faithful, and able God. You have permission to dream and do the thing that makes you come alive because—good news—it's not up to you! *He* is able to accomplish it through you when you wake up and choose surrender. This book is my humble petition for you to say yes to the assignment God puts before you and to do it in a way that leads to your flourishing and benefits your people.

Abide, Deny, Obey

Are you worn out and sporting a side cramp by the amount of striving you've been doing? Do you feel like you're stuck in a bad dream, trying to run a race but going nowhere? Are you beginning to wonder if this treadmill you've been on is really God's best for you? Do you feel worried and anxious about whether the effort and time you're giving is worth what you're receiving in return? I've been there time and time again, working hard for the Lord only to find myself with questions and burnout. I've found through trial and error that the problem is not God, but us. When we try to build something on our own that was never up to our own ability, hustle, or strength to build it leaves us tired and no closer to our destination. In fact, our part in the building of this whole thing is meant to be light. Does it require hard work? You better believe it. But it is not a weight we carry on our own backs. If we are willing to read the instructions a little closer, we see a better, more fruitful, more life-giving way of going after our dreams.

I need to be totally transparent with you. I won't promise that this book will make you feel good and like a total boss babe. In fact, I can almost guarantee it won't; I'm not out here trying to boost your ego. My intention is not to make you feel capable of anything. A good morning routine and a gratitude journal might be helpful along the way, but it's not what will bring you the fulfillment and clarity you are searching for. I'm a "say it to your face" "not going to beat around the bush" type of gal, so I'm going to lay it out for you straight. Here's the path we are taking together in this book. Try grinning while you read the next few sentences to help lessen the blow.

The path of abiding like our life depends on it.

The path of denying our own leadership.

The path of learning surrendered obedience.

Abide. Deny. Obey.

Sexy, right? No one ever accused me of being a motivational speaker and I'm not about to start today.

If somewhere along the way we find ourselves famished and lost, we can turn back to God's path and follow Him. Our path promises potholes and a faulty GPS, but God's way leads us to our destiny.

God the Creator is the one responsible for these beautiful and evolving dreams and passions within your heart, and He has already given you in His Word the tools and resources you will need to achieve them. It's past time we threw away the idea that our assignment comes with a Happy Meal prize of popularity and adoration. We are no longer measuring success with outward gain. Not anymore, friends. Now we are trekking a new path where God's glory is our highest gain. Our yes to His will, His pace, and His path is our theme song. Full stop.

Your yes: that's the first step this journey requires and an intentional choice we will make every day for the rest of our lives.

Taking God's Path

Trust me, taking the shortcut is never worth the early arrival when it comes to God's plan. Jesus' path and His pace will always be better than any other path, regardless of how green and pretty the scenery. Every time, those tempting off-roads lead to nothing but disappointment, emptiness, and a sense of needing more, more, and more. I'm tired of doing it my way only to be left worn out and disappointed. I say enough is enough.

I'm going to bring to the table what I believe to be the greatest hindrance to us walking fully in our God-given dreams: we aren't quite ready to toss aside our own ideas of what our lives should look like. This idea of *denying* our own will is too much. We can't give up being the one in charge. We've said the prayer, showed up to church, and put the Christian stamp on whatever project or ministry we start, but ultimately, we are still in the driver's seat. We haven't learned the Jesus way of denying ourselves and following Him.

Slowly, if we aren't watchful and discerning, we can become so overly confident in our own ability, status, and giftings that we forget to build the character necessary for us to sustain that place God brought us to. Our humility, surrender, and dependence on God can quickly turn into a false self-confidence, a need for control, and dependence on our own giftings and charisma. This is the very nature that needs to be put to death through the power of Christ for us to truly be disciple makers, world changers, and dreamers with God. Only through the daily death of our own fleshly desires and through the resurrected life of Christ in us can we partner with the Holy Spirit to build God's kingdom.

The tension between living for the glory of ourselves and the glory of God is where we find burnout.

This isn't the way we were meant to flourish. We were never meant to rely on the praise and admiration of others to grant us access to the table. The Trinity doesn't just say, "You can sit with us," but rather, "You belong with us." We were never supposed to live anxiously when joy and grace are at our disposal. Instead of sitting and resting in the seat God has already reserved for us, we are frantically running laps around the table. We can stop striving, take our seat, and enjoy the portion our good Father has already prepared for us. When we get comfy and settle into God's will for us, we can be women who begin pulling out seats and ushering in more to sit down beside us.

I want to make one thing clear. God loves that we make beautiful things. I'm all for cohesive color schemes and cool logos. God our Creator loves seeing our creativity poured out in forms of stunning book covers, moody photography, and inviting spaces. Give me scripture mugs and a trendy book bag any day; I'm here for it! And I can bet you that God is cheering from the heavens when we gather together for conferences, worship gatherings, and mission movements. I believe this is a powerful way to spread the good news of the gospel far and wide.

The foundation to the dream, the ministries, the goals, and desires of our hearts must stem solely from the roots of an intimate relationship with God and worship of Him alone. Just like you can spot a tree by the fruit hanging from it, the world will see who you behold by the fruit in your own life.

As we begin to tackle the fears and doubts that can hinder us from saying yes to the assignment God has placed in our heart, I pray that we will find the courage and joy to give God our wholehearted yes. And as we begin taking steps of obedience toward that dream, I pray that we will not rely on the broken path that leads to false promises, but that we will choose a better way to dream with God.

There *is* a better way, my friend. And this book will continue to point us back to the gospel. That is where we will find the way to fulfill the purposes on this side of heaven that God appointed for us to do. He says that His yoke is easy and His burden is light. This is still true for us today. This beautiful thing that God has placed in your heart is meant to glorify God, serve others, and help you grow in relationship to God. It will require hard work, but the good kind of hard: the hard that builds faith and sharpens our character. No more low hanging, spotty fruit for us, sister. We're going after the long-lasting, good for the soul, life-giving stuff.

As we say yes and build on what God has called us to do, let's remember it's not ours to build. Not by our efforts, but by our obedience and God's ability. Are you ready to go after this dream in your heart in a better way? Me, too. Let's get to work.

A Permanent Spiritual Address

I was a real-life shapeshifter in my youth. Every year I would magically turn into a completely different person with a new personality, hobbies, the whole deal. First was "punk Lexi": let's call her Lex, because God forbid anyone mistake her for anything other than what she was: edgy. I chopped my hair, wore dark eyeliner, and decided to start a band in my garage. *Jesus, fix it.* Any time I uncover a picture from this era collecting dust in an attic box or pasted with gum in a junk drawer, I take it home and hide it in my closet.

The worst part of this era was the fact that I was the drummer in said band. At fourteen, I spent my birthday money on a red drum set we picked up from someone on Craigslist. I can hardly type this out from the embarrassment I still carry to this day. I want to take this moment to publicly apologize for the sheer agony I inflicted on my neighbors, parents, and siblings— *forgive me.* Drumming was not my spiritual gift and someone older and wiser should have told me to stay in my lane.

Not long after that, I entered my flirty, preppy stage—a stark contrast to the wannabe-Avril Lavigne stage I had just gone through. This is also known by my close friends and family as the Lindsay Lohan circa 2006 era. I was tanning, wore too much bronzer, and painted my lips pink. Everything was pink. To be fair, it was the early 2000s, and were you even anyone if you didn't have a pink Razr flip phone?

Last, and definitely the most humiliating, was the "missionary Lexi." You wouldn't find me without rope sandals, a Nalgene bottle, and a cross dangling around my neck. I wore long skirts and thrifted T-shirts, because if people in third world countries didn't have Abercrombie & Fitch, why should I?

I owe these sudden changes of personality and look to the fact that I have always been the type to become like the people I hang out with. If someone has a slightly unique laugh, I will start to laugh like them when we are together. Accents of any kind are a danger zone for me. While binge watching *Downton Abbey*, I called my husband "Lord Josh" and most of the furniture in my apartment was antique. You get the picture.

There is a definition for this madness, and it is called the social proximity effect. I read about it once in an online article and it stuck with me. The social proximity effect says that you begin to look, act, and take on the mindset of those you spend most of your time with. Simply put, the company you choose affects the person you become. I would go as far to say some people even begin to physically look like someone they are with all the time. Have you ever seen a couple that has been married for years and they actually look alike? Let's be honest, I've seen people start looking like their dogs, too.

As an adult I've noticed I can quickly begin to mold into the type of women I spend the most time with. Or when I'm at the gym (OK, fine, on my couch scrolling social media), I'll catch myself being influenced intellectually and theologically by the content I'm consuming. Maybe it was more obvious in high school when the clothing and attitude and verbiage were so distinct, but we are all prone to conforming into the people around us, even if those people are writers, actors, or influencers. We become what we behold.

God, who designed the very nature of humanity, the process by which we live and breathe, think, and act, knows more about how we tick than our brightest minds here on earth. Jesus, being fully God, knew the importance of our proximity to Him. He understood the value of relationship and the transformative power that comes with sharing space, time, and relationship with Him. His invitation to us to dwell with Him, abide in Him, walk with Him, and to be a disciple of His is evident all throughout Scripture.

What does abiding have to do with chasing dreams and saying yes to God?

Everything. Absolutely everything.

Examine Where You're Dwelling

The path God has for you will only make sense and be fruitful if you are abiding in Him. For good measure, let's define the word *abide* so we are all on the same page. Through a quick search on dictionary.com the word *abide* means "to remain; continue; stay, to have one's abode, dwell." Keeping the definition in mind, I want us to park on this verse in John 15:4, "Abide in me, and I in you. As the branch cannot bear fruit by itself, unless it abides in the vine, neither can you, unless you abide in me" (ESV).

If we look at the biblical meaning of *abide*, we find that, according to Strong's Concordance, the Hebrew word for *abide* in the Old Testament is יָשַׁב – *yashab*, meaning a shared habitation, to marry, to share space. It goes as far as taking that connection with someone to making that person a *home*. The Greek word in the New Testament for *abide* is μένω – *menō*, meaning to stay, remain, be continually present. Jesus is asking that we not only remain with Him, but that we make Him our permanent home, our spiritual address. Gosh, I love that.

As we spend more time with Him in prayer and in His Word, we will begin to become more like Him, just like Lex became like her edgy friends. The most beautiful part is that because we are created in His image, the more we become like Him, the more we step into who He created us to be. Through simply abiding in Him we are walking in our purpose. It may not always feel as productive as running on empty and posting inspirational quotes on social media, but it builds our character and identity more than anything in this world could.

When we choose to make abiding in Jesus the main thing, good fruit is a natural progression. Remaining with Christ and being transformed by the renewing of our minds through His presence and Holy Word will change our whole life. Something so simple, but it often takes us years of trial and error to learn. The methods and systems culture has promised will make us fulfilled and successful haven't held up. The secret sauce isn't found in a bullet journal or online course—it's found in abiding in God's presence. In order to produce a life that brings glory to God and serves others, we must first be sure that our allegiance is to Jesus Christ alone. Beholding Him and building a personal relationship with Him is the bread and butter of this aim. We cannot go and point people to the Father when our lives are pointing to idols we've been abiding in instead.

It's time we take a good, hard look at our life and take inventory of the fruit we are producing. Taking inventory allows us the opportunity to see where we are being influenced, and it reminds us of ways we can actively form our spirit to be in alignment to God's. Does our fruit look like being slow to anger? What about having self-control and patience? Does it offer others kindness, gentleness, and love? Are we people who fight for forgiveness and redemption? Do we carry deep joy and peace as we walk through trials? None of us have this down pat. I certainly do not. Because we will always fall short when it comes to being, well, perfect, we submit ourselves to the grace of God. Only through His grace, friends. But this is why inventory is good work. We can see where we need more of the grace and Holy Spirit to do a work in our hearts.

Second question to ponder—where are you abiding? Who has your attention, adoration, and time? Who are you learning and gaining wisdom from? Who are the people and resources that you are giving authority to in your life? Maybe your inner circle is crummy and needs a revamp. And not to be the one with the church answer here, but does Jesus hold space in your day?

Our Thoughts Become Our Home

Similar to the social proximity effect is the power our thoughts have on our physical bodies. The mind and the body are so deeply connected to one another. What we allow our minds to dwell on, we tend to feel physically. Fear is such a clear example of this at work. Fear and worry left free to run in our minds will affect our bodies as well. Have you ever experienced this? I sure have. Lack of sleep, loss of appetite, and even severe pain in our bodies can be a direct response to the state of our thoughts. Have you ever been so worried about flying that you can't eat? Maybe you've waited for the test results from a doctor and it kept you up at night. When I'm dwelling on the fears of the "what ifs" my chest feels tight and my stomach hurts.

The correlation between mind and body is studied far and wide. But God has already revealed to us in His Word how to be transformed by the renewing of our minds through His power and Holy Spirit.

Quick, important note here: I am not speaking about clinical mental illness. Mental health problems are real and need professional help to overcome in many cases. I am an advocate for therapy and have invested in it myself. There is a spectrum of mental struggles that can and should be met and treated respectfully.

Sometimes we need extra care of our minds just like we need extra care when we break a leg, contract a virus, or get a cavity. What I am not saying is, *if you only had more faith, prayed more, or believed more you would experience freedom from all mental health issues.* In some cases God does heal people in a moment, but that is not everyone's healing journey. Jesus *and* therapy can absolutely be the path to healing and restoration that God has planned for you.

What I am talking about is *not* mental health issues per se but the day-by-day fears, worries, and negative thoughts we allow to fester. The thoughts that we continue to give power to are where I want to focus. I want to make that clear. OK? Moving on.

What we allow to take dominion over our minds will determine our thoughts and our actions. We default to being led by our feelings and allowing them to be our ultimate guides. We follow our heart at a whim and rely on it to be our greatest compass. (This mostly works in Disney movies and rom-coms.) But we are cautioned in Scripture not to rely on the whims of our heart but on the guidance of the Holy Spirit. Not only that, but we are instructed to be transformed by the renewing of our minds so we can have wisdom and discernment. Our minds are the central place of spiritual change and transformation, the headquarters of our decisions and actions. Paul knew this when he wrote:

> *Do not conform to the pattern of this world, but be transformed by the renewing of your mind. Then you will be able to test and approve what God's will is—his good, pleasing and perfect will (Romans 12:2).*

How easy is it to conform? Look around—it's so tempting to morph and mold into the women that we believe we need to be in order to do God's work. But Scripture tells us that transforming into the version of the women that society is pressuring us to be is not the way we are called to do work in God's kingdom. Trends come and go faster than skinny jeans and boy bands, but the transformation that comes with being made holy through Christ lasts forever. Conforming leaves us stagnant and paralyzed, but a renewed mind in Christ through abiding in Him produces long-lasting character and eternal transformation.

In Philippians 4:8 we are instructed to *think* about, "whatever is true, whatever is noble, whatever is right, whatever is pure, whatever is lovely, whatever is admirable—if anything is excellent or praiseworthy—think about such things." It is safe to say that if what is coming out in our actions, words, and choices is noble, right, true, pure, and loving then we are linked to the truest and most authentic source of these attributes.

If the sum of our thoughts are an indicator of where we hang out spiritually, then our thoughts better be planted and rooted in God, who is true, noble, pure, right, and all things holy. Do you see the link here? Sticking close to God produces good and holy thoughts and actions.

On the first day of school this year my eight-year-old came home with the school motto printed on a piece of paper. It read,

Thoughts become words,
Words become actions,
Actions become habits,
Habits become character,
Character becomes your destiny.

While this isn't straight out of Psalms I feel that it supports so accurately what the Bible has already said about the link between our mind, body, and actions. What occupies space in our thoughts will rear its head in our real-life bodies, relationships, and lived experiences. What seeds are we planting in these brains of ours? Are we being intentional about planting seeds of goodness and truth? Because if we are, those seeds will bud and sprout and blossom into all kinds of wonderful flowers that will be a sweet aroma to God and a blessing to others. Seeds of holiness will bloom hope and faith and joy. This may be a start to a less anxious and overactive mind. Who doesn't want that?

Our thoughts can be the little beginnings of the God-dream we have been given. The very start of our first simple yes to His calling.

Let us not forget that transformation begins in the mind, and the way to that transformation is through the spiritual act of abiding in the True Vine. Our brains have formed pathways and patterns built by our thoughts and experiences, and when we submit our thoughts to the authority of Jesus, we begin to rebuild those pathways. God is quite literally transforming our minds physically and spiritually. As we are transformed, we will be able to test and approve, as Scripture says, what is God's good, pleasing, and perfect will. Our thoughts will become more sanctified through abiding in Jesus, and those sneaky thoughts that entertain fear and doubt will be tossed out with the garbage. As we put on the mind of Christ and submit our processing to Him, our desire to co-create with God and live lives that are in obedience and service to Christ will flourish.

Spiritual Formation

Did you know that on average we have 6,200 thoughts every day?[1] We are constantly being informed about the world, people, how we should feel, what we should think, and how we should respond, and we are processing that information constantly.

---

1   "How Many Thoughts Do You Have Each Day? And Other Things to Think About."

This input forms us spiritually as well. Spiritual formation is happening whether we intentionally inform our own spirit to be in alignment with God's Word or not. Our ideas about life and purpose, our beliefs about God and His desire for people and the world, how we respond to fear and suffering are all being formed based on what we allow to form us. This is why spiritual formation is such an important part of the Christian life. It's why being intentional about abiding in Christ and staying close to Him is crucial to who we become.

Let's touch on a couple ways we can daily position ourselves to abide in Christ and actively influence our spiritual formation. I believe studying God's Word is a direct way we can get to the heart of Jesus and know Him deeper. I am absolutely not talking about rising before the sun and having your nose deep in the Word. I don't know about you, but in my real life my kids have a sixth sense of knowing the exact moment my eyeballs open in the morning, and they are at my bedside asking for snacks moments later. For most of us, the early morning "quiet" time is a myth. Does that serene scene actually happen outside of stock photos from a Google search of "daughter of the Most High"? If I had a dollar for every time I had an uninterrupted, peaceful time with God, I would have a whopping zero dollars. But abiding *is* possible. God had mothers and parents and working people in mind when He asked us to abide in Him. So how do we start abiding in the middle of our lives, right now, today?

Turns out that abiding in Jesus is not a place we go. Wherever we are, God is there, too. We don't have to go anywhere special, light a candle, or crank up the worship playlist to summon God. Candles, worship, and quiet are good things to create an inviting space, and abiding can totally look like this. In fact, it looks like this for lots of folks. But the good news for the dear ones who can't always get that extra quiet space is that God is always with us, ready to connect right where we are in the middle of any season.

With that being said, the Bible is an irreplaceable source of knowing and loving God on a deeper level. If we can meditate and be learners of Scripture, our maturity in Christ will grow leaps and bounds. Reading God's Holy Word is a direct source to learning about His character and nature. Jesus instructs us in Matthew 22:3 to love the Lord with all our heart, soul, mind, and strength. Our heart and mind are both equally needed and capable of loving God.

It's second nature for us to love God with our emotions, don't you think? But, goodness, we have a strong mind between those ears of ours, and how wonderful it is when we love God with that, too. As disciples we are called to be life-long learners, studying the nature and character of our Teacher and Lord, Jesus. For some, this means making a whole career of it and spending lots of time and energy in a school of theology. But I promise that you can be a disciple right where you are, whether at home tackling laundry and breastfeeding, or pursuing your career and everything in between. We are all called to be theologians, knowing and understanding God's Word as a way of worship and relationship. And knowing and believing you have permission to be a student of God's Word will be a precious tool as you form your own views of the world.

There is no right or wrong way to consume God's Word. My personal favorite at this point in my life is pairing Bible reading with podcasts. We have the gift of so many wise, faithful, and biblically literate men and women out there who have been called to speak and teach God's Word through podcasting, and it has been such a gift to me. The best part is, I can do this while sitting in the carpool lane or shopping at Trader Joe's, so it's a double win.

One of my most recent favorite things to do is simply Google a character study on a man or woman in the Bible and consume all the data I can about them. Suddenly they become so human to me, not just a name on a page. When we pay attention to the time period, the cultural influence, and social status of these people it helps us not only interpret Scripture more accurately but understand their struggle and purpose.

We live in a time where we have so much access to the Bible it's ridiculous not to utilize it. Push through the idea that it must look a certain way and simply start somewhere. What your time learning looks like now will be different in a year, in five years, and in twenty years. Lord willing, one of these days we will make it to the land of quiet hours with warm coffee, but if that's not your life, don't throw out the baby with the bath water. Find a way that works in your life and go for it.

A great companion with being in God's Word is prayer. It even says in 1 Thessalonians 5:16-19 to pray without ceasing and to give thanks in all circumstances. To pray without ceasing is to set our spirit in alignment with God's Holy Spirit and to be in a continual posture of prayer and worship as we do our everyday errands and responsibilities. It's a continual *muttering* in our spirit offering praise, thanksgiving, and conversation with our Heavenly Father. I see it as an ongoing dialogue in the spirit. As things come up in our day, big or small, we utter our worries, excitement, prayers, or seek wisdom from God. This invitation to pray without ceasing is a precious aspect to our relationship with God and an indicator of His intimate love for us. Praying without ceasing is simply staying connected to God through communication. Not leaving Him out, but actively engaging.

Prayer has many ways of presenting itself and we can tap into its multifaceted expressions depending on the moment. One thing that stays the same is that prayer is not just how we ask for God's intervention but how we abide in His presence. Just as we use communication to grow closer to those we love, we communicate through prayer to draw near the Father. God, who is omnipresent, is seeking a continual muttering to Him, of engaging with Him, lifting up small praises, releasing our worries, inviting Him into every moment. He is all in when it comes to being active and present in our everyday lives.

Reader, we don't need to be told we have the spiritual gift of intercession or wear a prayer team lanyard to pray. We just don't. Prayer is for the Christian and anyone who desires to find communion with God, in all seasons and circumstances of life, *especially in all circumstances.* You and I can meet with God, even if it's not polished and neat.

Jonah prayed in the belly of a fish (Jonah 2:1), Daniel in a den of lions (Daniel 6:10), Jesus prayed in the wilderness (Luke 5:16), Peter prayed on a rooftop (Acts 10:9), and Paul and Silas prayed in prison (Acts 16:25). There is nowhere that we can pray that is absent from God. Today, during the sixty steps I took from my car to my front door, I said a prayer. Anywhere, at any time, that's the gig.

Let me say this. We might be having a conversation about chasing dreams and doing the thing God placed in our minds to do, but that alone is not the reason we abide in Jesus. We abide in Jesus because He is worthy of our worship, space, time, and relationship. Jesus offers the very purpose of life itself—a relationship with Him. He is the abundant life we have today and have hope for in eternity. He is too good not to choose. The Lord Jesus who moved into our neighborhoods, was rejected, killed, and then resurrected and is sitting at the right hand of God, and who is interceding on our behalf is worthy of our devotion.

You have the free will to choose where you abide, and I'm crossing my fingers and saying my best prayer that you will choose to make Jesus your dwelling place. I pray you pursue proximity between you and Christ, choosing to share space, time, and relationship with Him.

For all of us, I hope that as we live our normal, beautiful lives as people who look a little more like Jesus every day, that our posture, choices, and intentions point directly to the Jesus we abide in. That the way we love and welcome and make space for those around us will be a holy representation of the God who loves, welcomes, and makes space for each of us in His presence. My deepest hope is that you say yes to making Jesus your holy place of residency, and as you chase your dreams they will be grounded in the True Vine and produce good fruit.

Let's make His presence the place where we stay, remain, and dwell now and always. Let's get near to Jesus and stay there, make a home, splurge on nice throw pillows, and put down a welcome mat. Let's make a permanent spiritual address, plant the seeds, and watch the garden grow. The path God has for us will lead us to places we never imagined we would go, but if we abide in Him, we will always feel at home.

CHAPTER THREE

Everyday Obedience

I was sitting in a cozy corner of my favorite coffee shop in a district called Waterlooplein in Amsterdam in late 2018. I had my notebook, Bible, and hands down the best caramel latte I have ever had. Listen, I don't know what it is about European baristas, or if they are harvesting magical beans over there, but regardless, I swear to you that coffee is better in Europe. This is a hill I will die on.

I rubbed my hand around my large, pregnant belly settled between my thighs. The moment I'd conceived my third child my belly popped out instinctively. It was like, Well, we know what to do! I still had four months of growing and stretching and bloating ahead of me, and yet I was already getting comments like, "You're due any day now, aren't you, honey?" and "Are you sure that's not twins in there?" from random strangers. No, Susan, this is just my five-months pregnant belly and the double cheeseburger I just scarfed down at lunch, thank you.

It was December, and you know what that means. Every Midwestern millennial in America was gearing up to reveal their word of the year on Instagram. If you aren't familiar with the sub-Christian-culture phenomenon that is the word of the year, then let me enlighten you. And just for clarification, I'm totally into this. I have a word every year, and yeah, I realize it's mostly women in their mid to late thirties who do this but I'm a woman in my mid thirties so let me be. The word of the year is a word God gives you to serve as a guidepost, a sort of pretty banner if you will, that you gear your decisions, intentions, and expectations toward for the coming year. Many people find it helpful to have a word that helps them stay focused on a specific discipline or value they will intentionally foster during the year ahead. But it can also be a word that is a prophetic promise from God for your life and what you hope to experience.

For example, I knew someone who once said God gave her the word *flourish*, and that the year ahead would be one of new and exciting possibilities, her dreams would start to come true, and she would develop this superpower to turn anything she touched into gold. I embellished the last part, but you get the point. Others said their word was *delight*, and that the year would be full of things that brought them joy and happiness.

The previous year my word was *abide*. I spent a lot of time that year being intentional about being with God, making that spiritual address a permanent one like we discussed in the last chapter. I was eager to see what God would do in this next year.

With two toddlers who ate their boogers and left a trail of destruction everywhere we went, a baby on the way causing me immense heartburn, and a fast-approaching move back to America from Europe, I was all in for some flourishing and de-light. I was so ready and eager to hear what God would say, and let's be real, my hopes were way up there. *OK, Holy Spirit, I'm here and I'm listening. Give it to me. What is my word?*

I looked around at the chattering coffeeshop dwellers, sipped my latte, and picked up my pen ready to jot down what He would reveal.

Then...

"Obedience."

You have got to be kidding me.

"No," I mumbled under my breath and leaned back in my chair.

"Yes," He insisted.

I was really hoping for *flourish* or *delight*, but I would have settled for their cousins, *peace* and *joy*.

I was coming up on six years of full-time ministry and had a lot of experience in the "go where you send me" kind of obedience. What I was learning was that obedience also meant our everyday obedience to God's Word and leading. Obedience, as I would find out, was the doorway, the only path to the abundant life that Jesus talks about in John 10:10, and it would be the very thing I would need to relearn and continue to pursue as I dived deeper into the assignment God had for my life.

Obedience. There it was scribbled at the top of my notebook: no turning back now. As soon as I wrote it, I noticed something I'd never noticed about that word before. Right smack in the middle of the word *obedience* was the word *die*. *Great*, I thought. *It can only go uphill from here.* I circled the three-letter word that was so clearly there protruding out in front of me, demanding to be noticed.

As I began to focus in and look a little closer in the days and weeks after, it was obvious that for me to live a life of obedience to God would mean that I would need to learn to "die" or "deny" myself in the process. A humble reminder that would serve me well. God's path for our purpose isn't always going to lead us to scenic destinations. Sometimes the path looks pretty monotonous but it's important to keep walking in obedience and finding the beauty and power in the mundane.

Hear and Obey

I am a mom to three little girls, all under the age of nine. While they each have their own strengths, hear me when I say they all, especially my three-year-old, struggle with quick obedience. Every morning is the same routine. She comes into my room, wide eyed, big smile, happy to see me and cuddle. The moment I ask her to do something she doesn't want to do or tell her no, her whole demeanor changes. She goes from, "I want to spend time with you and I love you, my adoring mother" to a full-on Western standoff.

She faces me, hands on hips, of course.

Eyes narrow in on mine. The nerve, y'all.

And then the questions begin to fire.

"But why do I have to?"

"Can I do this instead?"

"Can I do it later?"

"Why does she get to and not me?"

Or if she's feeling really spicy, it's a hard deadpan, "No, Mom."

Motherhood has tested me, humbled me, and given me a tangible experience of what the biblical meaning of *pruning* feels like. I've been around the block a few times dealing with the stubborn toddler who just doesn't want to do what they've been told to do. I might not be stomping my feet around the house, but I sure have squared off with God one too many times when He has asked me for my yes in obedience.

Say this with me: *shama.*

Shama is the Hebrew word for *obedience.* In Strong's Concordance it's translated to mean "to hear, to listen, to give attention, to understand, to submit to, and to obey." In Hebrew the word *obedience* means two things at once: to hear and to obey. They are one in the same; there are no buts, whys, maybes, or nos sandwiched in between them.

When I began to study up on the topic of obedience and why it is so near and dear to the life of the Christian, I couldn't skip over John 10:27: "My sheep hear my voice, and I know them, and they follow me" (ESV). It's a classic, the verse you will find in a tiny gold frame in the bathroom at Grandma's house. Don't let the sweet analogy fool you—this verse is a foundational pillar for us as disciples.

Hear and obey, hear and obey.

Hearing God isn't always that easy, especially when we have so many other voices competing. Did you ever play that Sunday School game called Shepherd's Voice? It was a complete disaster of a game, but us wild kids ate it up. The brave and willing adults would put a whole bunch of us, blindfolded, in the middle of the room. *I mean, come on.* Then we would each have a partner who was not blindfolded somewhere in the room calling our name and giving us instructions of where to go to find them. The purpose was to practice what it can be like when we have many conflicting voices and messages in our lives while wanting to follow God's voice.

For us to be able to discern and know God's voice from our inner voice, friends' voices, culture's voice, husband's voice, you name it, we must start with abiding in the Vine. We went over this already, but only when we are abiding in Jesus are we going to learn to hear and recognize His voice over all other voices. Sure, it might be a sloppy mess at first, but it gets better. We sharpen our ability to know His voice quickly. I'll tell you what, if I hear my daughter Emma cry in a room full of kids I will immediately know it's her; I'm her mom and I know her cry. Same with our relationship with God. The closer we are with Him and the more time we spend with Him, the quicker we will recognize His voice from others.

In the English dictionary the definition of obey is "to comply with or follow the commands, restrictions, wishes, or instructions of." When Jesus calls us to walk in obedience, He is offering a new way for us to live, move, and operate in this world. Instead of being led by our own will, we are now submitting our will to Him, making ourselves obedient to His voice. This is the nitty gritty, secret sauce of pursuing our God-dream. If we can get this part right we will experience God's plans for us to their brimming capacity.

Our choice to obey will be defined by what we believe about God. If you think about it, what we believe about who God is and if He is who He says He is will be the catapult into how we live and obey and follow Him. If we believe He is good, all loving, merciful, and abounding in grace then choosing to follow His Word and His Spirit in obedient submission to Him will be a joyful obedience. If we believe God is a cruel, pious, unloving, unmerciful God who is ready to strike us at any moment, then yeah, who is going to joyfully obey that guy? Jesus says in John 8:31 (AMP), "If you abide in My word [continually obeying My teachings and living in accordance with them, then] you are truly My disciples."

As we abide, we know God, we build intimacy with Him, and through that relationship we develop the desire to obey Him as a sign of worship and desire to see His will be done. To be honest, this right here, the hearing and obeying God, is where the magic happens in our lives. It's the difference between a life lived in the natural world and a life lived fully and righteously. The answers to pursuing your dreams and succeeding in the things God has placed in your hands all boil down to this foundational groundwork. Will you abide in Christ, will you obey His Word and His leading, and will you deny yourself and follow Him? Without aligning ourselves in these three disciplines we will bear fruit that is from our own will. You want to know how to go and do the powerful work you have been called to without burnout, disappointment, and confusion? Get close to Jesus and stay put right there. Obey His Word, which is revealed to us in the Scripture, and daily deny the temptation to be led by self.

The Road of Sanctification

Abiding is not about simply doing the right thing and going through the right motions. It is only through sanctification of our self, our desires, our dreams, and how we live life that our calling will truly be what God intended it to be. Obedience is not just doing what is right, but it's doing what is right through the path of relationships, worship, and sanctification through the Holy Spirit.

Sanctification is a big Bible word that is loaded with incredible meaning. In 1 Peter 1:14-16 God calls us to be holy as He is holy, and sanctification is the process of being made Holy through Christ. When we are choosing to abide in Christ and obey His will from a heart of devotion we enter the road of sanctification, living our lives for God's purpose and design. Being sanctified through Christ is believing that our redemption has been accomplished through Jesus' death and resurrection on the cross, and that through faith we now live by the Holy Spirit, being transformed and sanctified to be more like Christ. Sanctification is a lifelong experience as a Christian. Every time we meditate on God's Word, every time we gather with other believers, when we worship and pray, it is all playing a significant part in our sanctification from old self to new in Christ.

When we are living from our own will and being self-led, we will produce a self-made version of the dream and assignments God had planned for us. Our dreams need to be sanctified through Christ in order to fully become what God intended. Only through sanctification can we see the purpose that God has over our giftings, passions, and calling. When we are living lives in the rhythms of pursuing sanctification, our dreams will go through the same sanctification process as well. It won't be what we can imagine for ourselves, what we hope, what we believe is best, but it will look like what God intended, dreamed, and planned for us.

This is the work that needs to be done to see good fruit in our lives. We can gain all sorts of head knowledge with devotionals, conferences, and attending all the Sunday services but still see no change in our life and character if we are not being transformed in the process. This is because abiding without obedience that flows from relationship and worship leads to a stunted growth instead of sanctification. When we respond to God with obedience from the root of relationship, the work of sanctification begins.

Sanctification is not done in the flesh but by the Spirit. We need the Holy Spirit alive and active inside of us to be transformed. This is the work we are called to, made for, destined for by God. Our true destiny will be lived out when our dreams are sanctified. How good is God that He isn't after us doing what He says out of fear but through love in a relationship with Him.

Obedience to God is the doorway to the full and glorious life He has planned for you. It won't always look like you imagined or show up when you thought or hoped, but it will be right because it will be His way. The good news of the path laid out in front of us is that our part to play in this journey is obedience to God and His part is everything else. When in doubt, obey His Word and follow the last thing He told you to do. I love the story of Noah because the guy heard God tell him to build a boat one time and then it was radio silence for four hundred years. I'm sure there were countless days when Noah was like, *OK, did I actually hear from God? Am I the loser and weirdo of the century?* But he heard and obeyed God.

Could it be that right now you are being called to long obedience? Is it possible that the space between you and your assignment is staying faithful to the last thing God said? Sometimes the next right thing is simply to stay faithful to the last thing.

That's the game plan. To be the kind of women who hear and obey because we don't doubt the leadership of God in our lives. We should be growing in the discipline to make hearing and obeying one and the same, and reset our vision on what obedience means and see it as an action step toward fullness and hope. We know one thing for sure: we won't have to wait four hundred years for the next step like our friend Noah.

Pursuing a life of deeper obedience is a generous invitation to an abundant life of knowing God. It was never about performative submission, lacking in relationship and purpose, but a life full of fulfillment, goodness, and holiness.

Deny Yourself

What is your knee-jerk reaction when you hear the word *obey*? Recently a friend of mine told me she has thrown out the word *obey* because it brings up past experiences of abusive authority in her life. To obey meant to submit to an ungodly and unloving power. For her, obedience has strongly been correlated to abuse. Unfortunately, I don't think she is alone in this experience. The word *obedience* today can often bring up feelings of spiritually abusive leaders who used the words *obedience* and *submission* to further their agenda or power. I get it, and I've experienced it myself firsthand.

Godly obedience has been muddled in the experiences of guilt and shame. The original design and desire for obedience, in its purest form, was and is a road map straight to the love and fullness God has for each of us. And the road of "denying yourself" that Jesus calls each Christian to only leads to the abundant life He promises.

According to Strong's Concordance, "to deny" can mean two things. "A" refers to relation to another person—for example, when Jesus said to Peter that he would deny Him three times before the rooster crowed. Peter denied having any acquaintance or connection to Jesus. The second, "B," is referring to what we are talking about now, that Jesus calls us to deny ourselves and follow Him.

1. to deny
A) to affirm that one has no acquaintance or connection with someone
B) to forget one's self, lose sight of one's self and one's own interests

This is what Jesus is asking of us when He calls us to deny ourselves and follow Him. The phrasing of "denying yourself" happens in a conversation that Jesus had with all twelve of His disciples as they gathered together one evening. We can tune into the end of this conversation in Luke 9:23-25, where Jesus says,

Whoever wants to be my disciple must deny themselves and take up their cross daily and follow me. For whoever wants to save their life will lose it, but whoever loses their life for me will save it. What good is it for someone to gain the whole world, and yet lose or forfeit their very self?

Let's be really clear about one thing when we are talking about denying oneself. This in no way diminishes your worth. God absolutely loves and adores you. He says that you are precious in His eyes, that you have been created for a beautiful purpose, He wants a relationship with you, He sings songs over you, He raises a banner of love for you, He knows how many hairs are on your head, for crying out loud—you were made in His likeness! He loves you and finds you worthy enough to come and die for you. This has nothing to do with your worth. Denying ourselves means letting go of the steering wheel, putting to death the things that do not bring honor to God, laying down the sinful nature in us. It means that our lives are lives for Christ, not ourselves.

Here's what I know to be true about people walking the earth today, specifically in modern America and other first world countries. We don't deny ourselves diddly squat. We have become so hyper focused on what makes us comfortable, happy, and secure that anything opposing that is quickly labeled as "toxic" or "bad." We gauge right and wrong by our feelings rather than spiritual fruit and holiness. To grow spiritually and into more holiness, it is necessary we experience the spiritual growing pains that bring maturity in our lives. The difference between growth and stagnant spiritual growth is our willingness to embrace the trials and challenges before us. Choosing to make decisions based on how they make us feel only leads us away from true growth.

What I'm saying is that just because we desire to do things, say things, or act in certain ways does not mean it's inherently good and beneficial. It might serve our desires in that moment, but the collateral damage that we cause without self-control, love, and all the other fruits of the spirit is immense. While yes, our emotions and bodies are gifts from God and serve us in so many beautiful ways, they cannot be our guiding compass to a full life. When our emotions, bodies, and minds are surrendered to the God who made them, they can function at their full God-given capacity and purpose.

In the pursuit of what we have been assigned to by God, isn't it so easy to let our own ideas, preferences, and will take over? I believe we all want to see God be glorified in and through the dreams He has placed within us, but we also have a nature that wants to do it our way. We can quickly justify allowing our own agenda and ego to run the show as long as we are still doing the thing we feel called to do. We choose to be directed by God but then we add our own spin on it just to stay in control. We can quickly enter a negotiation relationship with God that says yes to following Him, but under our own conditions. It can sound like this: "God, I say yes to you, under one condition…"

I don't have to move.
I get to stay in this relationship.
I don't have to surrender this one sin to you.
I don't have to change my lifestyle.
I get to stay neutral and non-confrontational.
I give you my twenties and I get the rest.
You bring me a husband first.
You heal me from my illness.

There are countless "conditions" we knowingly place on our walk of obedience to God and many more we discover as we choose to surrender deeper to Him. But the fact of the matter is the same: God is asking us to lay aside our conditions and choose to follow Him wholeheartedly. To deny ourselves is to deny the conditions we set in relationship to God and to the way He has called us to live. With conditions attached, our ability to follow Him is limited. It is through the laying down of our will that we have freedom to truly walk in the peace, joy, and fullness of promises and hope that Jesus offers each of us.

The Joy of Obedience

Have you ever felt guilty about enjoying your life? I'm serious. When we are faced almost daily with terrible and heartbreaking news from all over the world, it feels strange to go and have brunch with your friends. You receive a text delivering sad news of someone who is in the hospital, and then the next text is from Amazon alerting you that your matcha tea arrived at your doorstep. You attend a fundraiser for women and children coming out of domestic violence, and then you go home and watch a rom-com and order pizza. Life is weird like this. It throws us the worst and also the best. Is a life of surrendered obedience a life that yields only to struggle, trials, and solitude? Is it possible, and dare I say, God's will to hold the tension of both—challenges, sorrow, and trials, along with celebration, fun, and joy?

The Bible calls us to die to self, surrender our will, and walk in obedience to God. This is the way of the Christian life. And at the same time, God tells us to be joyful and do good... to eat and drink and find enjoyment in all the days He gives us (Ecclesiastes 2:24). And He tells us "a joyful heart is good medicine!" God instructs us to go eat and drink with a merry heart, and He means it. We experience so much healing, nurturing, and life through the act of spending time with others over food and drink. That food and drink can look like brunch and coffee or a bowl of punch and cake, and it can take the form of date nights with your husband, movie nights with friends, worship, and celebrating birthdays and babies and newlyweds. This is all good work. It is all ministry and holy obedience. And it is absolutely necessary that we have open arms to the mourning and gladness of life.

This life is a gift. We were meant to experience and live in the tension of the both/and. The tension of caring and feeling deeply for those in pain, and for rejoicing and celebrating with others as well. We are to mourn and weep, laugh and play. The Christian life is not a big sob story in which we suffer and cry and deny all good things for the sake of suffering for God. God is in the suffering just as much as He is in the backyard BBQ hangouts. He is in all of it and wants all of it for us. He is in all seasons, with us in every experience. Amen?

On the other side of the coin, as we submit our will to Christ, our desires will look more and more like His. As we deny our own way, we will find our will beginning to align more with His. Remember when we talked about how where we abide will be evident in our life through our words and actions? As we abide in Christ, the way we make decisions and live our everyday lives will reflect the will and desires of God for us. Denying yourself and following Jesus isn't forfeiting this incredible body and mind God Himself has given you. It means we are no longer the lord over our mind and body. We are denying our leadership and submitting our mind, body, heart, and soul to God's Lordship.

When we say yes to denying our own will for God's will in our life, it sounds a lot like this. We stop asking, "What do I want?" and start with, "What is God's best for me?" It looks like pausing before big decisions and inquiring from the Lord the way David did when he faced trials. It manifests in the way we handle relationships and how we enter challenging circumstances. It stops us from leading with our limited experience and knowledge and being led instead by God's perfect leadership.

Can I share a little habit that has served me greatly over the years? It's short and punchy, but it gets my heart and mind in the right framework before the day begins. Before my feet hit the ground, I pause at the edge of my bed in the morning and say this quick prayer:

"God, thank you for this day. May Your will be done and Your kingdom come in my life. I submit to your Lordship over my mind, my emotions, my heart, and my body today. Holy Spirit, help me to accomplish Your good works wherever I go and in whatever I am doing. Amen."

Saying yes to Jesus requires a daily and discerning no to self—passing over the leadership of our destiny to God. It's time to lay the foundation, friend. We must hear and obey, align ourselves with God's will, and choose His Lordship over our own.

If we can begin the good work of learning that joy-filled obedience to God is not a crummy, terrible, abusive act of self-denial, but a radical, lifegiving act that leads to abundance, man, won't we be better for it?

The abundant life Jesus gives is a fulfilled and intimate relationship with the Father. An eternal reward of being in restored communion with Him, forever. Abundant life looks like operating in the fruits of the Spirit, living closely with Jesus, and being filled with God's Spirit. Abundance is more intimacy with Jesus, more holiness, more sanctification, and deeper fulfillment. Abundance is what we get when we settle down in obeying God and walking His path. It's a well that doesn't run dry, a hope, peace, and joy that we feel to the bone.

Choosing to follow our own will and desires is rooted in building our own kingdom, but denying our will and choosing to submit to the Father is the Jesus way. Choosing to hear and listen to His voice and follow it, that is the Jesus way. Denying ourselves so that Christ can live through us and walking in surrendered obedience to the Holy Spirit is the path that leads to life. One thing is for sure: this path we are taking to chasing our dreams is going to require that we get comfortable with the uncomfortable. There's no way over the discomfort, no way under it, we have to walk right, smack into it.

In a world that preaches, "My will be done," will you join me in the Jesus way? Of proclaiming, "Not my will, but God's will be done in my life"? This world needs more women saying yes to building God's kingdom and not their own. As you step into radical obedience and joyfully submit all authority to Christ, your God-given dreams will become more than you could ever comprehend or imagine. With God as our source, all things are possible.

The Lies of Spiritual Real Estate

I've always known I wanted to be an author.

The first story I ever wrote was a riveting tale about a girl with lime green hair. I was so proud. Not long after that I would spend hours hiding away in my bedroom, staring into the screen of an ancient desktop computer, pounding away at the keyboards with my chipped white nail polish. I wrote on that computer for weeks on end and came up with a fictional story about a group of friends, all of whom had powers and were on a quest to save the world. I can still picture the detail of the landscape and hair color and quirks of each character.

I felt completely and unapologetically myself when I took pen to paper and let my imagination lead. It was at sixteen that my love for writing and my love for God found their way to each other. I decided I would write a devotional for other girls my age about their identity in Jesus. It was the first time I began to think that my writing could maybe, possibly be for more than just enjoyment, but for a bigger, deeper purpose. What started as a hobby quickly turned into a passion and most certainly felt like a sort of destiny.

That devotional that was going to change the lives of every teenage girl in America was never completed. We probably dodged a bullet there, let's be honest. And after the start and quick end to that I went on to have several failed attempts at starting a devotional for the next ten years. That's right, ten years. While

God was trying to plant a passion for an assignment meant for later in my heart, I was trying to force it to happen in my timing. I continued to write and fill journals, and found myself growing deeper in my passion for putting words on paper. But none of those projects ever came to fruition.

On an average day at twenty-seven-years-old while I was doing the normal changing of diapers and cooking of food, God said to me, "All right. That devotional you keep trying to write, it's time. Do it now."

I think my reaction was something along the lines of, "Uh. Ya sure, now? There has never actually been a worse time."

But it was right, and I gave my yes to God and spent the next several months writing *True North*, a devotional for the real-life mom. I wrote my first devotional for mamas, just like me, in the trenches of motherhood trying to pursue Jesus well. God's grace was beyond sufficient in my writing process. I wrote mostly while sitting on the floor with my two babies, toys scattered around me and the movie *Frozen* on repeat.

Things were going great at the start. I would type away and marvel over the fact that I was actually "doing the thing." It felt so good to be using my gifts in a way that I knew would help other moms. It was during the marketing and selling portion of the process that things started backsliding.

The spiritual real estate felt completely over-saturated. From the looks of it, it was full. What would my tiny input bring, anyway? It wouldn't make a splash, that's for sure. *I mean, what am I even doing here? Who am I to think I can weasel my way into this world with all these other clearly qualified and better suited Christian gals writing words and saying impactful things? I would only be echoing them. I would be a voice lost in the noise.*

Up until that point I hadn't been very involved with social media. I had no idea what a hashtag was, and the whole online marketing world seemed like something made up and exaggerated. I knew enough to know I needed to utilize the online space to sell my book, so I jumped right in to take a closer look around. Turns out this was not a made-up world and there were in fact thousands of real life people selling and marketing and starting businesses and the whole enchilada. It took five whole seconds for me to realize I had been living under a rock. This online space was thriving and occupied and I was equally inspired and mortified.

The worst of it was that I quickly became aware of how many women were out there doing the same thing I was. Women who were way more qualified, successful, and talented by a landslide. They were selling books, building their own brands, and writing and speaking about the same things I had written about. It felt like there wasn't space for me in this big, scary world I had become suddenly and widely exposed to. I was crushed and weighed down by so much doubt. My dream of becoming an author was sucker-punched by my unbelief.

Up until that point I had been confident and excited to write. I knew in my gut this was the thing I was supposed to pursue. But the moment I turned my gaze outward and climbed the mountain to get a panoramic view I saw just how many people were out there pursuing the same path. Instead of thinking, *Holy smokes, how cool is it that we are all in this together, working toward a great and glorious mission?*, I thought, *Well, crud. Just kidding, I think I'll see myself out and find a less occupied neighborhood.* I allowed my doubt to take place in the process, and unbelief began talking to me. It said nasty things like, "Why write if you're not the best? Why write when someone else is already writing the same thing? Why write when 'she' could do it better? The market is oversaturated, you missed it. You're too late to the game. Just give up now and find a different passion. God really let you down on this one, didn't He?"

I had clocked in years of writing and creating with God up to this moment, and comparison, fear, and doubt in God's assignment for me almost allowed unbelief to override my obedience. I learned through trial and error and what felt like a lot of wasted time that my path may look similar to someone else's but that doesn't mean my assignment isn't necessary and important.

Along God's path for your purpose, you may see that the area that He's called you to—whether it's writing, teaching, pastoring, or anything else—is already occupied by other people but that doesn't mean you aren't meant to be in that space, too. When we are walking God's path and living in our purpose, we should take on a mindset of abundance.

Abundance Rather Than Scarcity

Here is the honest truth about feeling like you're not the only girl out there doing what you feel called to do.

You're not.

Let me say it nicer.

It's not you, it's also everyone else?

One more shot.

Your assignment was specifically chosen by God for you to do, and He also put you in a wildly diverse and glorious team that will run with similar but not totally the same assignments as you. I repeat, you are on the same team, accomplishing the same goal but in different ways.

Does this make sense?

There will always be someone prettier, more talented, more qualified, more experienced, and further ahead than you. Your gifts and assignments are deeply important and given by God but you are not a snowflake or more important than anyone else. I repeat, you are not a superior child of God, His most favorite ever. We all are equally loved, there are no favorites in God's kingdom. In fact, the singular mission only works when we value the community mission. Together we thrive, together we succeed, together we can go the distance. There are lots of friends out there you just haven't met yet who have very similar assignments as you. But if you do your part and they do their part, together we bring God's kingdom and His mission into the world.

While you are not more important or special than the next gal, you do have a specific story, experience, and part to play in this world. It's both/and. We are called as a body of Christ to serve His mission, and individually we have specific assignments that only we can fulfill. We need your personal yes to God, your specific voice, story, and path.

Unbelief rears its nasty head in lots of forms. It comes disguised as comparison, causing us to be so focused on what everyone else is doing that we lose track of our road of obedience. It comes as a whisper, planting seeds of doubt as we wonder why the fruition of our dreams is taking longer than we expected. Or it comes as confusion, as we feel called to something but lack the answer to when and how our dreams will be played out. Unbelief is like quicksand, slow and deceiving, and a path that leads to the death of seeing our giftings and calling flourish.

No one gets to fly under the radar when it comes to experiencing unbelief and doubt. It's bound to show up in one or many forms as you say yes to God. Maybe you feel this way today about something you're pursuing. Can I give you a warm welcome to the club? You're not alone in this thing, and I promise you, even the girls you think have it all together feel the same way or at least have before. This is the human nature in us, combating faith with doubt, battling our reality with the spiritual ability and power of Christ in us.

What led to my unbelief was believing the lie of scarcity and its pal comparison. I climbed the dreadful mountain and took a long look around. I paid close attention to the differences between me and the other girls who were doing the same thing. I compared how they were doing it with how I was doing it. I decided for myself that there was no room for me at those tables and that my voice would be just a whisper in the already full arena. I disqualified myself from the room for fear that I was too late and too small.

Scarcity is believing there isn't enough to go around. Scarcity tells us that what we have isn't enough, what we offer is too small, that there is no more space for us. But God does not operate from a place of scarcity. He does not assign us to works that are oversaturated or filled up. He sends us right to the places we are needed, to the people who need us, to do the things He needs us to do.

Comparison is the Thief of Time

At the root of my unbelief was the mistake of taking my eyes off Jesus. As my eyes bounced left to right and up and down, comparing and measuring and evaluating, God was redirecting me back to His gaze.

When our eyes are on Jesus and we aren't acting like squirrels so easily distracted by who and what is around us, we will stay focused on our own journey of obedience. When our eyes are fixed on Jesus we are not questioning His goodness, His will, and His faithfulness. When we are fixed on our journey of obedience we become way less concerned with everyone else's. In fact, we start cheering others on and hooting and hollering for them because we know they are on our team, not our competition. God's mission for His people is not to be mistaken for another rat race. His kingdom isn't some enterprise. We are the Church and the Church is His bride.

Whoever first said that comparison is the thief of joy was spot on. How many times have we felt the joy sucked out of us over a project, business, or even being a mom from comparison? There will always be a steady flow of content out there that you can count on to distract you from your one, glorious life. Comparison has a supply chain that will never end.

Until we stop looking around and keep our eyes fixed on our path, it will continue to hold power over us. But joy isn't what comparison has stolen most from me—in my experience, comparison has been the great thief of *time*. Y'all, the hours I have spent idolizing another girl's life, all the good coming from her work, how successful she is, how clean and cute her home is, all of it. The time I've wasted throwing a pity party over what she has that I don't when I could have been enjoying the path God gave me is too many minutes to count. I regret every last second that comparison has taken from my family, my marriage, and all the good and holy things God has called me to steward. I say not a moment more of it.

Unbelief breeds comparison, doubt, and distraction in your spirit. There is no good thing that comes from unbelief in God's path and assignment. While you are on this path of pursuing the God-dream in your heart, you cannot take unbelief down that road with you. It just simply cannot join you. We are no longer going to climb a mountain to scope out all the other paths out there. We are no longer sacrificing our joy over the illusion that someone has it better. And we are absolutely not going to waste one more measly second of our precious lives to idolize someone else. Enough is enough.

Acknowledging and Surrendering Unbelief

Here's some gospel truth for you: God has set your path ahead of you, and it is *full* of all the resources you need to run it well. God has made it so clear to us that joy, peace, and fulfillment are all found when we abide in Him. And because He is faithful and good, He has a remedy to our unbelief. God has shown us in His Word what to do when we have unbelief in our heart. One of my favorite examples of how to handle unbelief is found in Mark 9. Jesus meets a man whose son is possessed by an evil spirit who has robbed him of his speech. The father, desperate to help his son, brings him to Jesus and the boy starts convulsing in response to the evil spirit being in Jesus' presence.

> *Jesus asked the boy's father, "How long has he been like this?" "From childhood," he answered. "It has often thrown him into fire or water to kill him. But if you can do anything, take pity on us and help us." "If you can?" said Jesus. "Everything is possible for those who believe." Immediately the boy's father exclaimed, "I do believe; help me with my unbelief!"*

I love this so much. I have been the father in this story so many times. I have been confused and angry that God would put something on my heart and I wouldn't see it happen. Or sad that I'm not further along in my dreams. I've had questions, and I've been in seasons of total loss of direction. What I've realized is this: there's no formula to avoid seasons like this. There's no guarantee you will skip failure, or disappointment, or grief. It's in these seasons that the enemy tries the hardest to shake our faith and our trust in God. It's in the storm of confusion that the enemy whispers, "God has let you down. You don't have what it takes. You missed it. It's too late for you."

I can't begin to express the importance of leaning into the character of God in these moments. When unbelief comes we can pray, "Lord, help me with my unbelief. I trust You and have faith in You." God is for you. God is working on your behalf. God longs first for a relationship with you and then to partner with you in His mission. God has placed dreams in your heart for you to pursue for His glory, the good of others, and to your benefit.

When our unbelief in God's character begins to trump the truth of who He is, the enemy has a hold on what God has already set free. If you're searching for purpose, don't let your unbelief become your guide.

We can learn from the dad in Mark 9. We can simply ask Jesus to help us in our unbelief. Be honest about where you are. When unbelief comes knocking, turn to Jesus and be honest about your doubts and fears. We can turn away from searching within for understanding and ask God to step in with His perspective. We can acknowledge that we will fail if left to our own devices but succeed when we seek the power and grace of God and ask Him for supernatural belief to override our circumstances and feelings.

When the sand begins to quicken, self-help will only drag us further in. Instead, let this be our mantra,

Help me, Lord, with my unbelief.

Help me not to rely on what I see or feel, but in Your Word and character.

Help me trust in You over my doubts and fears.

Help me give You my yes, even if it looks different than what other people are doing.

Align my spirit with Yours.

There will always be a "better," more "qualified" girl in the room by our measures, but God has a place for you. We will always be faced with questions that fill us with doubt, but God is trustworthy and faithful. Unbelief will always try to kill the dream God has assigned to you, but He is always there to help you override unbelief with faith.

Remember yourself as a child who knew, loved, and created with God in total freedom and security? May we live as children, never questioning if we have a seat at the table, if what we do matters, or if what we have to offer has a special place in God's story. May you say yes to God as a child does when they feel safe and loved and whole, leaving no room for doubt or unbelief to tarnish the gift of co-creating with God on the beautiful mission He has placed within you.

God's path for your life and purpose will likely not resemble the life you would have created for yourself, but we are promised that His path for us will be far better than we could ask or imagine. Giving God our yes doesn't mean we'll go down the easiest, most pain-free path—in fact, it often requires lots of hard work and consists of various trials—but it does guarantee that we will go down the most fulfilling path that will allow us to glorify God with our lives. When we abide in Him, deny ourselves, and follow where He is leading, we will find ourselves much less concerned with becoming someone, growing our following, and making a show of what God has called us to. Quietly walking the path God has for us this season is the most restful and fruitful way forward.

PART 2: POSTURE

ADJUSTING

OUR APPROACH TO

OUR PURPOSE

Start with Yes

At the awkward age of fourteen, I went on my very first mission trip to Chattanooga, Tennessee. Fourteen-year-old Lexi was really into *"Jesus is my Homeboy"* T-shirts and puka shell necklaces. I owned an array of Christian CDs featuring Switchfoot, Third Day, and Relient K, all of which I played nonstop on my Discman.

I was homeschooled, born and raised just off Route 66 in Tulsa, Oklahoma. I did attend a Christian private school for a whole two weeks in second grade, until one day my mom showed up at recess and yelled to me from across the fence, "Lexi! Let's go home, I'm gonna homeschool you!" This was after I had come home the day before announcing that I was in Spanish class, only to find out I was being taught how to speak in tongues from a chalkboard. So homeschool it was, and I loved it.

The ecosystem of my adolescence was within the walls of my home and also my church. I grew up in the Methodist Church, soothed by the sounds of organs and liturgy. The large majority of my early life experiences were molded from my time in youth group. These were my people. I lived for Wednesday night pizza parties, game nights during the fall, and pool parties and city scavenger hunts in the summers. If you know, you know.

Chattanooga, Tennessee, was my first-ever middle school mission trip. A full week without my parents, sleeping on church gym floors, pulling all-nighters with my friends? I was living for it. I was just stepping out on my own in this big world. Even as a naive teenager, I was (and still am) a control freak. I make to-do lists and tell people what to do like it's my job. I have items like Post-it notes and ballpoint pens on my Christmas list. As the oldest of three kids and an achiever to my core, I spent a portion of the long bus ride dedicated to, I kid you not, planning out my life. I put my earbuds in, played Switchfoot, and pulled out my journal and pen.

It read something like this…

Go to college at Florida State University.

Get a tennis scholarship.

Travel the world and make movies.

Become a writer.

Study counseling.

Marry a super gorgeous guy and name our babies Elizabeth, McKenzie, and Sophia (in that order).

I distinctly remember looking over my list and feeling really darn good about the whole thing. This was a good plan and God would absolutely approve. Bless my little heart.

One evening during the trip, I was sitting in the basement of the host church. I clutched my Bible and notebook in my lap, avoiding eye contact with anyone who could summon me to the front. Suddenly, I heard the Holy Spirit speak to me. It wasn't audible, but it was clear as day.

"Lexi, will you take out that list you made?" God asked.

I took out the list. I was half prepared for the stamp of approval and pat on the back from God for my incredible life planning skills.

"Will you throw it away?" He asked.

Ouch. I went still, waiting for the, "Just kidding, it's perfect!" to follow.

"I have more than you could hope for or imagine planned for your life. Above anything, I want you to surrender your life to Me, serve Me, follow Me. I will always be there with you, walking this whole life by your side. I have so much love for you, and I want to be your closest companion. Will you give me your life and serve me? Will you follow me?"

Cue the tears. Lump in throat. Chills down my arms and down to my toes. An overwhelming sense of love and safety consumed me.

"Yes. *You have my yes,*" I replied.

"Just keep pursuing me, and I'll take you where you need to go. Trust me," He instructed.

It was the moment that changed everything for me. I can't write the words without a lump in my throat and chills down my arms again. He is inviting us to surrender our whole life to Him and gain His undying, ever-present, wonderful, perfect companionship. He is so personal and good I can hardly take it. Jesus has not left my side from that moment in that basement of that random church in Chattanooga. The worst of them and the best of them. He is the best of every single good and holy thing I have experienced on this earth.

We all have assignments from God, but none of us know how His plan for our lives will play out. When we try to flesh out the details for our assignment from our own desires, we end up with something far less powerful and purposeful than what God has for us. Your posture toward your assignment needs to include open hands that hold your ideas of how your life will play out loosely because God has a better plan for you than you could possibly imagine.

You Have My Yes

Three years after I spoke with Jesus about following Him, we had another conversation together. I was sitting on a rooftop in the Dominican Republic at a mission base, sticky from the humidity and heat, this time a senior in high school. I'll admit it, I was up there trying to get a glorious tan. I mean, who wouldn't if they were in the Caribbean? I was lost in my own thoughts, looking out at the rooftops that stretched far in front of me, Dominican merengue music coming from the streets below, when it happened just as suddenly as the first time. Jesus asked me again, "Lexi, will you follow me? Will you serve me with your life?"

"Of course. You've had my yes for three years now. I'm all in. I just want You."

"Will you serve me, even if it means leaving your family? Even if it means not having financial security? Even if you're scared and lonely? Will you trust me with your health, too?"

He'd upped the ante. It had started with "follow me" when I was fourteen. Now the question held a bit of weight. Why would He bring up all those "even ifs"?

I hesitated.

"Yes. *You have my yes.*" My response came out more as a question than a statement.

A string of yeses after that moment led me to spending six months in the mountains of the Dominican Republic learning about who God is and how to share Him in remote places. It led me to hostels in China at eighteen years old, working with underground churches and teaching English. My small steps of obedience brought me to the base of earthquake zones, to single moms struggling in Haiti, to the mountains of Switzerland, to the villages of Brazil, and to living on the cusp of the red light district in Amsterdam. It was wild.

In 2012, Josh and I were married in a barn in Oklahoma surrounded by mason jars and an ungodly amount of twine and lace. We were settled in our little apartment in my hometown in Tulsa when God asked me and Josh for our yes to live in Europe and work with a discipleship ministry. We said yes, and that led us to six years of working with a team, leading training schools, and being the pastoral care for leaders in Switzerland and Amsterdam. We grew our family far away from our own families, and the yes was tested. Loneliness, heartbreaking homesickness, and unrelenting fear came, but God was so faithful when we said yes to His path and His way. I learned the beauty of sanctification through obedience and experienced the love of God in the middle of hardship.

We've been all over the world together, God and I, on small acts of obedience step by step. My yeses haven't always led me to adventure and comfort, but often into times of struggle and discomfort. But here is what I know for sure: God is who He says He is, the God with us, Emmanuel. He is the God of peace, the protector, faithful and true. He doesn't break promises, turn His back on us, or give up on us when darkness comes. Not even when we are dummies and think we know better.

The thing I always liked most about the story of Jesus calling Simon and Peter to follow Him was how they were just doing normal life stuff when He showed up. They were like us, working, going about their daily routine, making school lunches, switching the laundry to the dryer. Jesus surprises us, meets us in our most uneventful moments, in our most unimpressive seasons, and even at our ugliest kindly asks, "Follow Me?"

The first time we hear the voice of God inviting us to follow Him, the moment we accept Him as the one true God of our lives, is the first yes we give Him. It can look like a radical conversion of going headstrong down a path of rebellion against God, only to be saved and turned right side round with Jesus. It can look like an altar call at church camp when you're eight, or anywhere and everywhere in between. There is no testimony too big or too little that is not worthy of sharing and honoring. Whatever your story, that first yes is the start of a life of communion with the triune God and the beginning of a decision to follow His way, His path, and His kingdom.

Follow is a verb. I learned this from a billboard while driving down the interstate, and it really stuck with me. To follow someone requires action, movement, and active and intentional movement toward something. As Jesus followers, we are committed to following the leading and teachings of Jesus. In other words, we watch, listen, and study His movements, words, and actions, and we go about our life doing the same as He does. This is not a trend we jump on and hop off of when something shinier and cooler comes along. This is a now and forever decision to live by faith as a disciple of Jesus in obedience to His will.

Great Commission

But how do we follow someone who isn't physically here? How do we lock arms and ask questions and learn in the intimate way the disciples did with Jesus now that He is no longer walking among us? They had it so good, right? Imagine with me for a moment what that would be like. For starters, it would be *fun*. I refuse to believe Jesus was all business and no play. I bet you He was healing the sick and multiplying fish and the next moment causing all kinds of tomfoolery. There would be inside jokes, banter, and all sorts of shenanigans happening. I bet He would love my wit and see my femininity as a strength, not a weakness. Obviously, He would be the best listener. And along with the gift of His wisdom and insight at our disposal, I know He would have a contagious laugh. The kind that makes your belly ache and temples hurt. It would be the best.

We might not be able to literally laugh with, touch, and see Jesus today, but we have His Spirit with us all the time. We have everything we need today in these bodies in the places we find ourselves to follow Him just as passionately with our mind, body, soul, and spirit. How do we do this? We open up the Bible, the sixty-six books all put together that we call the canon, that is oozing with the very essence of God's character and nature. It's all right there, every page declaring His power and grace and holiness in this world and the one to come.

This incredible call to follow God echoes all the way back to Matthew 28:19 when Jesus says, "Therefore, go and make disciples of all nations," calling us as followers of Jesus to go and do His will. Remember, *follow* is a verb. It isn't only about *believing* in Jesus but becoming like Him through the transformative power of the Holy Spirit and active participation in His mission.

The Great Commission is God's mission statement for His Church. We read of Jesus passing on His mission to twelve of His closest disciples. This was His clear instruction on how they could continue His work in the world now that they said yes to Him. It says,

Then Jesus came to them and said, "All authority in heaven and on earth has been given to me. Therefore go and make disciples of all nations, baptizing them in the name of the Father and of the Son and of the Holy Spirit, and teaching them to obey everything I have commanded you. And surely I am with you always, to the very end of the age" (Matthew 28:18-20).

There you have it. What are you called to do in this life? This. This right here is our calling as people who have said yes to Jesus. This is not a calling saved for the most followed on social media, the pastors, the world-renowned worship leaders, or, dare I say, even the missionaries. It's for all of us. Every single one of us who is following Jesus and doing life the Jesus way, this is our banner. We are all called to go therefore and make disciples, baptize new believers, and disciple others in the teachings of Jesus. This is the call of all Christians. If you're like me and have a "what am I supposed to do with my life" moment every now and again, we can refer back to this. Our calling is first and foremost to love God and go and make disciples who love and are transformed by Him.

Josh and I were missionaries for six years and we traveled all around the world to disciple and preach the gospel. There were many times we were quite literally doing the "making disciples, baptizing new believers, and teaching them God's way" mentioned above. The way we introduce people to Jesus varies depending on culture, age, and circumstances. We are always called to live out the Great Commission as a Christian, but *how* we do that needs to be met with wisdom. Too many times have I witnessed well-meaning people preach the gospel in a way that only brought confusion, embarrassment, and disrespect to the people around them.

Gather close and listen here, friends: we have brains for a reason and we are to use them to help us discern good ideas. Sure, there may come a day when God might say, "Hey, Lex, preach from the hood of your car today at school pick up," but so far that hasn't been the vibe and I doubt it will be. Here is what I know is true. You have giftings put in your spiritual DNA, you walk with the aid of a powerful, helpful, and wise Holy Spirit, and you are capable of offering kind words, listening ears, hot casseroles, and your unique gifts every day to the people you share time and space with. This is kingdom work, gospel work, living in the flesh.

As You Go

The word *go* in the context of the Great Commission encompasses so much more than only one way of living out the Great Commission. *Go* translates to, "as you go." As you go about your life, as you go to the grocery store, as you take your tiny humans on a playdate, as you go to work, wherever you go, go as one who is following the leading and guidance of the Spirit of God. Wherever you go, go as one who follows Jesus. And He reminds us with the "therefore" that we can carry His kingdom everywhere we go, living out the will of the Father through the power of the Holy Spirit because He has already done the work to make that possible. Yes and amen?

The Great Commission is meant to be lived out in the spirit and flesh in active obedience to the Holy Spirit by the power of the Holy Spirit everywhere we go and in whatever we put our hands to. The Father sent His Son, Jesus sent the Holy Spirit, and we have been sent just like the twelve disciples. You and I are part of a far bigger legacy and purpose than we can even imagine. Your yes matters. Your yes is like the baton being passed from Olympian to Olympian, generation to generation. I just love that, don't you?

If the Great Commission is the mission statement then our assignment is the action plan.

We share a common goal but individually we will support that goal in thousands of different ways. Our calling is carried out right now in the messy, mundane, and uneventful moments of our lives. It is no small thing to bring the Spirit of God into our circumstances, homes, and workplace. How we show up in our everyday speaks volumes to the God we serve and what His intentions are for this world. As we go, living on mission, God may come in and surprise us with an assignment. It might sound like a flourishing desire deep in your heart that you just can't shake. Maybe you spot a burning bush on your evening jog. Have a crazy dream? Encounter an angel? Hear God's voice… like audibly? It's all been done before. No matter how it comes, don't dismiss it, embrace it!

We are going to set up camp around this conversation about assignments. We won't always call it "the assignment." See also, "the thing you feel called to do," "the dream," "your passion"—all of these work. So tell me, what is the thing you know deep down that you have been assigned to do? What I wouldn't give to hear you talk about it. Your assignment will change throughout seasons of life, but it's always like an itch that has to be scratched. It's holy, on purpose, placed within you by God. That thing, we are going to dig deeper into how we chase it, nurture it, and protect it against lies, burnout, and our own destruction. Before anything else, let's recall our authentic purpose: to embrace discipleship and to guide others in becoming disciples themselves.

The Bible is full of men and women like us saying yes to God. And just like us they didn't have all the answers, all the qualifications, or the full picture of where their yes to God would lead them. Think of Noah, Mary, Abraham, Ruth, Paul, Joshua, and so many others. None of them were saying yes to God with the understanding that one day their names and a part of their stories would be written in a book that would be passed around for thousands of years, read by numerous generations, and made into movies and Bible studies, or that they would be people we look to today for encouragement and wisdom. They said yes because they were following God.

When we start with saying yes, without all the "what ifs," "not nows," and "buts," God is able to lead us through the powerful work of sanctification through His Spirit. Along with our free will came our ability to say yes and to say no to God and His assignments for our lives. No is always on the table. If we use our free will to walk in obedience to Jesus and say yes to Him, we are telling God we choose His will, His way, His path over our own. We don't need to know all the steps or make it all make sense right then and there. Our simple but brave obedience opens the door to abundance in our lives and to the impossible. Obedience is our secret sauce; without it we never fully step into the fullness of what God has for us. So many good and holy things are waiting for us on the other side of obedience.

The assignment you know God has given you starts with you answering this simple question: Will you follow Jesus? Will you say yes to the assignment He has given you? I get it, saying yes isn't always a walk in the park, and it rarely comes without the occasional heartburn and minor paralysis. We don't need to know all the steps that follow, we just need to rest assured in the One we follow.

I'm saying this to me, and I'm inviting you to say it with me, too. Say yes to the dream, the passion, the project, the career, the next big step, whatever it is that God is asking for your obedience toward. We might see the big picture, we might not be qualified, and we might be scared to step out in faith, but if we just start with yes, God can lead us step by step. If we choose to take our belief and turn it into action, God will take our yes to places only He can. Let's say yes with open hands to following Jesus together in this one glorious life!

CHAPTER SIX

Walk with a Limp

It was on a Wednesday night at youth group that I experienced my first public speaking embarrassment.

The tables formed a "U" in the center of the room and my youth leader, Jay, sat in front. I was sitting at the table closest to the door. You need to know that at this point in my adolescence I noticed boys. I was totally into them. A big reason why I loved church so much at this particular time of my life was because I had a huge crush on a boy in my Sunday School class. I still know the guy, so to save both of us a little embarrassment I'll just call him Paul. I don't know any Pauls, so I should be good.

Jay asked all of us to open our Bibles so he could start the lesson. A few minutes in he lifted his head and, with a quick gaze over the room, said, "Uhhh, Lexi! Can you read blah chapter blah, verses blah to blah?"

I looked up in horror. A large lump formed in my throat, and I immediately began to shake. But I had to do it. I flipped to the scripture verse, stalling a bit, offering my poor body some time to ward off the onset of a heart attack. When I got to the verse, I could barely get the words out. As I started speaking I could feel my face turning bright red like a ripe cherry tomato, and then my whole neck felt hot. I felt all the eyes in the room on me, especially Paul's. *Why, God, did You allow Paul here tonight to see the end of my life as I know it!?*

I had zero idea what I read, and I didn't care. I just wanted it to be over, and when I finally stumbled through the last verse

I looked up at my teacher and could immediately tell he regretted asking me to read. Not because it sucked, which it did, but because it was obvious I was embarrassed and humiliated. The lesson went on, and I just sat there replaying the horror of what had just happened. I made a complete fool out of myself in front of all the girls and boys in my class. Eventually my voice calmed down and the nerves wore off, but I could still feel the heat on my chest. I looked down and saw that my neck was covered in red splotches. I could feel them all the way up to my ears and saw them disappear into my shirt. I was mortified. I knew everyone could see them.

I quickly began trying to cover them up using my Bible as a shield and pulling my hair in front of my cheeks so they formed a brown curtain over the sides of my neck. I wanted out of that room so badly but knew that leaving would only seal the deal that I was a complete dork. Eventually, by the grace of God, I felt the splotches go away and did my best to act normal as class ended. *God, never again, OK? Never let that happen again.*

But it happened again. It happened over and over and over again. It happened every single time I had to stand up in front of an audience and give a speech. The splotches appeared, like a blinking sign letting everyone know I was nervous and scared. As I got older the shake in my voice stopped, and I felt more comfortable sharing in a group, reading out loud, and sharing in large groups, but the splotches always showed up. They became my biggest insecurity. And it wasn't only when I spoke in front of crowds, but also when I was having a heated discussion, or talking about something I was passionate about. When my emotions were heightened, there they were, appearing like a rash that I couldn't cover up.

In my twenties while Josh and I were serving as full-time missionaries in Europe, I was put on the leadership team of the YWAM Amsterdam base. A few times a week we would sit together as a leadership team and hammer out lots of practical work, as well as prayerfully make hard decisions. Decisions that had a direct impact on real people and their real lives. It was messy and hard most of the time, but I really loved the job. What I didn't like was how in most meetings, given the fact that it was often emotional conversations and big feelings, my chest was splotchy and red. I would wear big scarves to cover it up or sink behind my laptop like a house behind a fence. Honestly, it was tiring. I was tired of always thinking about how I looked and how others would look at me and notice the rash. And for someone who knew deep down that she was called to write and teach *publicly*, this was a huge issue for me and occupied a lot of my thoughts when I was in large groups.

Sometime in the fall of 2018 Josh and I took our staff team that we led from YWAM Amsterdam to Germany for a staff training conference. Unlike most times in the past, Josh was on full-time kid duty so I could be part of the conference. I was elated. There is nothing I love more than learning and notetaking. I'm a firstborn Enneagram 3, the perfect storm for a good student. An older man who was teaching at this conference said something during one of the lessons that I will never forget. I don't think it was the main point of his lesson, and he probably wouldn't remember saying it if I mentioned it to him today. But he said, "Walk with a limp. You should live your life so dependent on God that if His Holy Spirit were to move away from you, you would fall over."

I know he was communicating that our lives should be completely dependent and interwoven with the Holy Spirit. I believe this with all my heart. And I know that his point was to remind us that every day we should spend time with Jesus, connecting with His Spirit and living our lives as an overflow of His Spirit. Amen and amen. But what the Holy Spirit spoke to me about on top of all these things was that I can't do any of the things God had placed in my heart without God. My insecurities, like the splotches that show up on my neck, are humble reminders that although I am wonderful because I am created by God, I am *not* God.

What he said resonated so deeply with me. Suddenly I was sort of, kind of OK with the fact that I have this awkward anxiety rash. My perspective on the whole thing changed: it was now a reminder that no matter how gifted or called I may be in something, ultimately it is by God's grace and the blessing and leading of His Spirit that it will add up to anything. My insecurities are the very areas of my life that God wants to come in and draw close to me. It is through my insecurities, my doubts, and my nerves that God wants me to lean into Him, become dependent on Him and His ability to impact others through my obedience. If I continue to believe the lie that I have everything I need on my own to accomplish what He has set before me, I am terribly, terribly wrong. It is God in me, and only God, that can take the giftings and dreams He put inside me and give it the anointing and blessing to make a fruit-bearing, long-lasting difference.

Your posture should be one of being so dependent on God that you would fall over without the Spirit's guidance in your life. By recognizing that we can't reach the fullness of God's plan for our life without Him, our posture will be one of dependence and humility, which will allow God to work through us in big ways.

Don't Let Your Insecurity Win

When Moses stood at the burning bush that never burned, God asked him to tell Pharaoh to free the Israelites from the hand of the Egyptians. The Egyptian people had been enslaved and God wanted to free them and bring them to the Promised Land. Moses knew the assignment, and he knew the calling God had on his life, but Moses had a speech impediment, and that inse-curity gave him doubt that he couldn't do what God asked him to do.

Moses said to God, "Pardon your servant, Lord. I have never been eloquent, neither in the past nor since you have spoken to your servant. I am slow of speech and tongue."

The Lord said to him, "Who gave you human beings their mouths? Who makes them deaf or mute? Who gives them sight or makes them blind? Is it not I, the Lord? Now go; I will help you speak and will teach you what to say."

But Moses said, "Pardon your servant, Lord. Please send someone else."

Then the Lord's anger burned against Moses and he said, "What about your brother, Aaron the Levite? I know he can speak well. He is already on his way to meet you, and he will be glad to see you. You shall speak to him and put words in his mouth; I will help both of you speak and will teach you what to do. He will speak to the people for you, and it will be as if he were your mouth and as if you were God to him. But take this staff in your hand so you can perform the signs with it" (Exodus 4:10-17).

God has been having the same conversation generation after generation with us. He is not concerned one bit with our insecu-rities, our lack of skill, our background, where we came from, or how gifted and talented we are. He is after people who are willing to say yes to His plans and purposes. Moses responds to God, who was manifesting as a burning bush in front of his eyes, about his insecurities and lack of skills. He saw his speech impediment as a bigger deal than what God could do through him despite his shortcomings. Instead of leaning into God, relying on Him to move through him, he tried to tap out. His insecurity won.

At this point I think God was pretty ticked. He wanted so badly to use Moses in this amazing story of freedom and restoration. I believe God wanted Moses *because* of his insecurities. When we are required to trust and lean into God in order to see the provision and the miracle, our own faith and trust in God grows. This was the perfect way for Moses to know God deeper and more intimately. God is never only about getting the job done but also about our process and our relationship growth with Him through the assignment. Moses was who God chose for this incredible mission, and Moses, too blinded by his own insecurity, wanted to turn it down.

So tell me, what insecurity is holding you back from fully saying yes to the assignment, mission, calling, mandate that God has placed on your life? Could it be a physical disability, speech impediment, or awkward nervous ticks? Is it feelings of insecurity about your past, the story of your life you are too afraid would turn people off if they *really* knew you? Might it be that you were told by a teacher or parent that you weren't good at the very thing you feel called to do? It breaks my heart to hear stories of friends who stopped pursuing their passions and what they believed they were made for, all because someone told them they didn't have what it took. That's the work of the enemy.

While our insecurities can hold us back or make us feel like we want to run and hide, I believe there is a real beauty in them. I've learned that while I strongly dislike getting that weird chest rash when I'm embarrassed and nervous, it pushes me to lean into God. It puts me in a position that keeps me humble and invites me into conversations with Jesus where I get to tell Him my worries and fears, and He gets to respond with, "I don't care about your insecurity. I am with you. Lean into my Spirit. Say yes, and I'll teach you every step of the way."

You Are Never Alone

I have a whole assortment of insecurities I carry around with me. I go up and down with loving and not loving my body, I worry about how people perceive me, I wonder if people think I'm qualified to write, *I* wonder if I'm qualified or even slightly good at what I love doing. I worry a lot about if I'm going to say the right thing, how I come across to others, and if it's OK for me to talk about the Bible and also listen to rap music and get frustrated with my kids.

That day in Germany when the speaker uttered the words, "walk with a limp," it changed the way I see myself. I know that the dreams God has placed within me are completely unreachable without partnership with Him. Every day that I set out toward my assignment from God, I am fully aware I am incapable of achieving His plans without full dependence on His guidance, power, and grace. If I want to walk this road without Him, I am relying on my own ability and limitations, but when I walk with a limp, leaning into Him, I'm now relying on His ability and lack of limitations. The devil wants me to give up because of my insecurities, but God wants me to use my insecurities as a reminder to lean into His ability.

When we try to be self-sufficient in living out the purpose God has for our lives, when we start running down the path leaving God in the dust, when the posture of our hearts blocks our ability to see how God is moving and hear Him clearly, then all we are left with is a half-built kingdom for ourselves that isn't helping anyone and is actually a detriment to our mental, spiritual, and physical health.

It is only when we realize that God is always with us and we come to see Him and depend on Him in every decision we make that we will be able to build His kingdom for His glory and achieve something eternal and meaningful in this life. When we realize He is with us at all times, our insecurities, embarrassment, and shame become opportunities for His love, grace, and redemption to seep in and create an incredible testimony of His power.

Imperfections Lead to Greater Dependency

So what does walking with a limp even look like? First, it looks like acknowledging you *need* God. Acknowledging that while we are wonderfully made and bear God's image, we need the Holy Spirit's guidance, grace, and power to accomplish His assignment for our lives. Then it looks like spending time with Him every day. Inviting Him into your inner conversations, asking Him for help and to have a teachable spirit. Spending time with God daily doesn't mean we always have our nose in our Bible; it can mean being in ongoing communion with God through whispered prayers and acknowledgement that His Presence is always with us. It's spending time intentionally to know Him better. It looks like being a woman who is so filled with God and saying yes to hard and big things that if He were to move, her whole life would change. I'm convinced this is the only true way to live. This is the way to abundant life, to a life that is full of peace, joy, and hope.

I know some people are turned off by the idea of living a life of dependency on God. Walking with a limp doesn't mean living your life embracing your weakness. It doesn't mean leaning on your insecurities like an abusive crutch. Walking with a limp means putting all your weight on Jesus, making Him your dependent, strong, and able foundation. It is through our leaning on Him that we stand strong. God is unable to fail you, lose His power, lose His ability to move mountains and part seas. I love how Ephesians 3:20 (NLT) puts it, "Now all glory to God, who is able, through His mighty power at work within us, to accomplish infinitely more than we might ask or think."

God's invitation to you is this: "Would you say yes to me? Would you trust that despite your insecurities, your limits, and your ability, that through your yes I will be with you the whole journey, teaching you what to do each step of the way? Would you spend time with me, lean into my unfailing, dependable, strong, powerful, and able Spirit? What I have in store for you is exceedingly more than you could ever imagine for yourself. This abundance of life is only found through me. Would you say yes to this life with me and to the calling I have placed inside you? So you have insecurities, shortcomings, and rough edges—so what? Where I am taking you is not dependent on you but my grace alone. I am God, limitless, able, and so ready to give you the grace you need to run this race well."

Walk with a limp. That's my best advice for you today. Lean into the Holy Spirit as your guide, strength, and power. He and only He can take you with all your insecurities and pitfalls right to the very places and to the very people you are called to serve.

It's in the marriage of leaning on Christ and standing firm in who He is that we shift our focus from our "lack of" to the God who lacks nothing. I'm still Lexi, the girl who was humiliated that night in church, who wanted to hide her insecurities. The difference now is that the more I am aware of my weaknesses and shortcomings, the more I am in awe of the One who chooses me anyway. What a relief that it doesn't all come down to me being perfect, but that my imperfections lead me closer and deeper with Jesus.

"Here I am" and "Yes, Lord" are all that is required of us. In spite of our quirks, God is still choosing us to do His work, and He is still faithful to take us by the hand and show us how.

Your Kingdom Calling

L et me stretch your brain for a second. Did you know that while your grandmother was pregnant with your mom, your mom had all the eggs she would carry in her lifetime? You, my friend, were one of those eggs. You were just a seed of a promise, planted in your mom during utero, who was being carried by your grandmother, who was also a seed of a promise in her grandmother once upon a time. It goes on and on. Isn't that the coolest thing? Which means—and this is too cool—that while a woman is pregnant, she is carrying two generations. And as a whole, three generations are represented. Wow. If you're a girl mom like me, I look at my kids in a new way with this knowledge. While they are running around in diapers, coloring on my walls with markers, and tossing spaghetti noodles on the floor, they hold the next generation in their tiny bodies. The next generation is there, with us, waiting for their turn.

This blew me away. And let's not forget, this isn't just a little person in there, oh, no—these little planted promises of the next generation hold a host of dreams and passions. They each have a plan and a purpose, with a whole story of their own waiting to be lived. These wild little eggs will become real life people who will have real life experiences and make their very own way in this world. They may fall in love, they may be the president, they may very well invent something super cool or finally resolve the issue of fitted sheets and how to properly fold them. Someone will call them their best friend, they will celebrate and dance, mourn and hurt, and face mountains of their own.

What about them? Have we thought much about those to come next? Do we make choices and see the world in a way that benefits and impacts the little souls full of purpose and dreams that will follow us and go beyond us when we are gone? And for the record, the next generations are not only the ones that may come from you, but those who are impacted by the ones you love well in your lifetime. We all have great impact and purpose in bringing up the next generations and running our leg of the race before it's their turn to shine. I think of the youngsters all around me who are kids of my friends. These tiny humans and their friends, and the kids in Sunday School and pre-K and the ones who call me Auntie that I have no blood relation to, these kids will take my baton one day.

The passing of a baton is no little thing. Have you watched the Olympic runners as they sprint full force on the track? As they make their steady and fierce final stretch around the curve they don't stop as they pass on the baton. They run with full ambition and determination, arms out, giving it their all for the one who is waiting for the hand off. For some of us it might be hard to imagine ourselves in this analogy because... running, ew. But spiritually, this is us. Second Timothy 4:7 says, "I have fought the good fight, I have finished the race, I have kept the faith."

In Christian circles we tend to do one of two things. We either see ourselves as meaningless, worthless, nothing without God, or we see ourselves as super special and important and everyone should be so happy they get to encounter our greatness. I feel like there is space to be humble in our place in God's kingdom without diminishing the beauty and value we have as God's creation. We are image bearers of God: "Then God said, 'Let us make mankind in our image, in our likeness, so that they may rule over the fish in the sea and the birds in the sky, over the livestock and all the wild animals, and over all the creatures that move along the ground'" (Genesis 1:26).

And in Romans 8:17 we are told that, "we are heirs—heirs of God and co-heirs with Christ, if indeed we share in his sufferings in order that we may also share in his glory."

And John 3:16 tells us that God loved us so much that He gave His Son to die for our sins, so that we could have everlasting communion with Him.

Our value as God's creation and position in His kingdom go hand in hand when we understand who God is and who He says we are.

This being said, what you do matters. Your life matters. Your walk with Christ matters. You are an image bearer, a co-heir to Christ, and loved deeply and perfectly by the Creator of the Universe. I let out a big "I'm over this" breath every time I hear someone say, "Well, I'm just a mom, what I do in my everyday life isn't making that big of a difference," Or, "I'm just a wife, what can I really do?" This kind of talk is a disservice to the role and authority you have as a co-heir of Christ. It's also the aftermath of believing that a "small life" is not a life of purpose at all. You should not wilt because your life feels small but instead embrace the invitations of faithfulness within the small world God has placed you in. Living a small life does not mean it is inconsequential. Stand up straight and flourish where God has you.

Can I tell you that most people will live small lives? Only a very tiny percent of people live a life recognizable by the world. A small life is not small at all. In fact, a small life is a life we should all desire in many ways. It is within the small, ordinary life that the most surprising things happen. It's the lives that are faithful, humble, and so deeply connected to family and community that have the longevity to seep goodness and good fruit for generations to come.

A Purposeful Life

What a lie we have created that a larger life equals a more purposeful one. The truth is a purposeful life is one that is lived faithfully to God. I will not change my mind on this. Faithfulness to the course set before us, responding to the duty of being an image-bearer in our own small lives is the greatest act of obedience we can give God. He is looking for the ones who are faithful in the small to carry out His most important assignments.

Because there is no such thing as a person with no purpose, and because there is no such nonsense as a life of faithfulness being small in value, we know one thing for sure: *You are a leader, and your yes matters.*

As we are trucking along in life doing our very best and saying yes to God our choices without a shadow of a doubt impact the generations that will come through us long after we are gone. Your yes to the audacious and brave God-dreams that burn inside you have been in motion long before you were out of your mother's womb. You are part of a legacy of women who, good or bad, left their mark on the next generation. Now it's your turn, you have been given the baton, handed the next length of the race. Will you say yes to the path God is giving you? Will you pave the way for the women who come next to do the same?

Whether we love the thought of it or not, someone, somewhere is watching the choices you make, the words you speak, how you respond to hardship, what you behold, and how you choose to live. We don't get to walk through life believing our little life isn't important. The people in your sphere of influence, whether that is your local barista you know by name, your co-workers, your family, or your clients, will know what you love by what you behold. We are not responsible for their choices and actions, but we sure can influence and encourage them or show a better way by the way we choose to live.

You know who also lived small and quiet lives and to whom God said, "Hey, you, I've got something in store for you"? So many women just like you and me throughout history and in the Bible.

Many women in the Bible had the moment each of us had to say yes to Jesus. They each came from women who had their own legacy and story to the place of it being their turn to impact their story and the ones after. I always think of Mary, mother of Jesus. This teenager, Nazarene girl, called to carry, birth, and raise the son of God. She said yes to this mysterious and joyful calling and through her obedience Jesus came, God on earth with us.

Fast forward to today, my mom, who is not written in the Bible or known around the world, raised in Tulsa, Oklahoma, said yes to Jesus as a child one day with no Christian heritage to name. Her yes led to diving into God's Word, prayers that were only heard in heaven, and small acts of obedience that led to me. Her yes allowed me to be born into a family that knew God. I was raised around prayer, worship, and discipleship because my mom and dad said yes to Jesus. This is legacy, played out in real, mundane life. The kind of life that moves and shifts family lines and generations ahead.

This grand world is full of women saying yes to Jesus in small ways every day. I know women right now who are walking in obedience in different capacities. Women who are saying a brave yes to healing the generational mental health issues in their families. Showing up day after day to therapy, doing the hard but meaningful work. This will change the lives of those watching, those bearing witness, and the lives that are not yet born. There are women who are showing up boldly in their yeses by moving their families to another state by the prompting of God. They believe the relocation is about them, which it certainly is, but do they know it's positioning their children for their calling as well? There are women standing their ground and fighting for their marriages. Women saying yes to showing up every day to be a mom when they can hardly get out of bed. Women starting a seed of a business because God said go for it. All these subtle steps of obedience will start a ripple effect and turn into a glorious wave of revival for generations to come.

You are not small. Your yes is not insignificant. Your decision to stick with it and say yes to Jesus day in and day out is the least small thing you will ever do. You have the ability through your obedience to lead every person watching, whether that's up close in your home, at a distance, or those not yet here. Your yes matters. We lack the imagination to comprehend what those small yeses will lead to in their days or in the days of women to come. Our faithful yeses of obedience are seeds planted one by one that with time will grow and produce great fruit.

Words have power, but actions are the proof of what you say. I believe our obedience to God is a real and honest "no-beating-around-the-bush" way of saying to others, "God is worth my yes, He is worth the risk, the sacrifices, the surrender. Look what He has done through my simple yes to Him, what a really good God!" Your yes gives other people the courage to give their own yes. Your yes shows others, "If I can, you can, too!" Your yes might be the push someone else needs to finally go all in. Your yes can lead her to Jesus, to her calling, just like someone else's yes led you to yours.

Leadership Isn't Personality Dependent

Your yes to God isn't just about you and your calling. The impact of your obedience doesn't stop with you and your story. Your yes to God is just as much for your own destiny as it is for so many others. I'm willing to bet that if you take inventory of your life right now, it is because of someone else's yes that you had the courage to surrender and say your own profound and unique yes. Maybe it's through this book and my yes to the obedience of writing it (I do hope so!). Maybe it's watching your friend begin their journey of fostering. Maybe it's your siblings who said no to addictive behavior that gave you the courage to say no yourself. Maybe it was the yes of your teachers, friends, parents that has placed you where you are and given you the desire to say yes to Jesus, too.

You have been led and you have been called to lead. Being a leader doesn't take a certain personality type or skill set. Being a leader takes a sensitive heart toward God, hearing and obeying His leading, and staying faithful to His purpose and will.

Have you ever thought that you just weren't made to be a leader? Somewhere along the way we have come to believe that only the loud, outgoing, big personality types are the leaders, and if you're more quiet, less loud, and introverted then your place is simply to follow. I want to debunk this theory. Leadership isn't only for the ones on the stage, leadership is a call to every single person, all personality types, all stages of life. What that looks like and how that is done will differ, but the truth of the matter stays the same: we are all leaders, we are all leading and influencing.

When I look at the stories of obedience in the Bible and imagine the thousands of stories that are undocumented, I notice that God uses people of every kind of background, ability, and personality. He loves taking the weaknesses of people and turning them into their strengths. When He called Moses, Joseph, Ruth, and Esther, He didn't care if they had the leadership ratings on the Myers Briggs test. He cared that they were willing to obey Him.

You guys, your leadership has nothing to do with your personality type. It has everything to do with your obedience. God has given you the personality, giftings, and passions you have for a reason and purpose. He could have made you any way and He chose you to be the way you are. There is absolutely nothing you lack when you are simply willing to say yes to God. If you hesitate to step into your calling because you have believed you don't have the personality it takes to achieve your goal I want to take that lie and send it back to hell where it belongs.

The Great Commission was for every one of us, including you. God is not looking at you and saying, "Well, darn, we can't use this one. She doesn't have the personality or natural talent for it." He has called me and you to go, go forth into the work of making disciples, loving others, bringing the good news to all. What does that look like in your life? What has He placed on your heart as your purpose in this mission? It starts with obedience, obedience in the small and in the big, obedience whether you think you have what it takes or not.

Who does your obedience impact today? Take a moment to think of their faces. Let the impact of your obedience sink in for a moment, and let it be a reminder to you that this isn't just about you and your thing. This is about so much more. Such greater and bigger and deeper things than you can comprehend.

As you go forward in this journey of obedience I want you to take with you the truth of these two things. You are a leader. Your obedience matters. You are not small, replaceable, or unimportant in this story of sharing Jesus with the world. You were created the way you are on purpose, and on purpose you have been given a calling and a destiny. Your obedience matters deeply, and with God you can literally change the world.

People of Mess

With all this talk about legacy and the importance of our yes to God, I know there are those out there who, like me, have royally screwed up. We have made big mistakes and made big messes in our lives over and over. We have hurt people, broken relationships, disobeyed God, sinned in all sorts of ways, and spent years of our lives serving ourselves over serving God. I want to speak to you, dear friend, who believes that her life will not leave a legacy of God but of destruction. Your mess isn't too big for God. Your mess doesn't have the final word in your story and your legacy. In fact, our biggest messes are the very things that God will use to restore our relationship with Him and bless others through the ministry of our testimony.

Testimony is our recall of God's great goodness and mercy in our lives, the witness on earth of a Heavenly God who rescues, nurtures, loves, and fully redeems each of us. When we sing His praises, at any stage of our lives, in any capacity that we can, there is no limit to what God can do with our song of praise.

In the Bible, the spiritual giants we look up to were people of mess, were victims of sin, faced socioeconomic disadvantages, and had troubling personality traits and character. Joseph was sold into slavery and abused, yet God led him to become a ruler. Moses had a speech impediment. Job lost everything and went bankrupt. Samson was reckless with women. Rahab was a prostitute facing a destructive future. Jacob had a history of deception. David committed murder. Peter denied Christ. Eve disobeyed God. King Saul was intent on killing Christians.

Your story is not too far gone to be used for the glory of God and the very good of others. I think about the dark days of my life when all the light seemed to be gone. I would wonder if God was able to redeem my mess like He had for others, and He did. But not only that, He has placed my feet on solid ground and sent me right into the stories of others in the same kind of darkness. This time I have a light in hand and hope on my tongue, and I can show others how Jesus is not done with them yet.

The hardest parts of your story are going to serve as God's greatest ministry in your life. He will redeem every wrong, every broken thing and make them right again. Your legacy encompasses all parts of your story—the days of joy and the days of despair. The echo of praise and testimony that your life sings will be the seeds of blessing and fruit in the generations after you and to all those who are witness to your life.

Your yes matters. Your mess is not too far gone. You are a hope bearer, a testament of the goodness and faithfulness of a living God. You are a leader because you are a disciple. Don't for one second underestimate the power of your yes.

Let's lace up our shoes and run our leg of this race with full-on gumption! This is our one shot, our big moment to live lives overflowing with the grace and love and joy of God. His path for us is good, purposeful, and will continue beyond you for generations to come. Who knows who is waiting for you on the other side of your yes? If I run my part, and if you run yours, we can see this thing to the end. Stretch those legs, grip that baton, and get serious about the race set before you.

Character over Charisma

I grew up in Tulsa, Oklahoma. Tulsa has been given the nickname Tornado Alley. Ever since I can remember a siren would ring every Wednesday at twelve o'clock sharp. The test alarm would give off a low to high vibrato—*wwwooooo, oooohhh*—for a painful three minutes. Everyone ignored it and grew accustomed to it, unless it went off any time other than Wednesdays at noon.

Like Californians are used to earthquake drills and Floridians are used to hurricane drills, we Okies are used to tornado drills. We are the people who respect the power and possible destruction of a tornado, but also marvel at its beauty. We watch from our front porches as storms calm and the sky turns an array of pinks and grays. We say things like, "A storm is brewin'" when we hear thunder rolling in the distance.

During our family visit to Tulsa this past summer, I woke up in the middle of the night to a huge flash! *Lightning.* The familiar rolling of thunder came billowing in. *A storm is brewing,* I thought. Soon enough it was raining buckets, and the tornado warning sirens began going off, humming up and down as they do.

I wanted to watch, so I slipped out of the bedroom to the big window in my parents' living room. Mom was already watching and Dad was pacing outside, looking at the sky. The weather app said there was one-hundred-mile-per-hour wind. The strange thing about this storm was the wind never circulated. It came in one direction, one hundred miles per hour. We watched as the two massive trees in the field in front of our house bent in one direction all the way to the ground, and then completely uprooted. I had never seen wind like that. Trash cans flew down the street several feet off the ground and went banging into cars.

The next morning, in real Southern fashion, we all went out and looked at the damage. The kids climbed the massive, uprooted trees and marveled at their large, thick roots. Neighbors emerged from their homes to check on each other and begin to help clear what debris they could.

What blew me away was how the two largest and tallest trees were completely uprooted while the smaller trees nearby stayed upright and intact. *How does this happen?* There are two reasons why trees are uprooted in storms. One, a weak root system. Two, being overly top heavy. The large trees looked strong, but the roots were dying under the surface. The trees were also top heavy; reaching so high in the sky with the weak foundation made them snap under the pressure of the storm. I noticed a third reason why the large trees did not survive and the small ones did. The soil around the big trees was near the road. They were planted in faulty soil. Large rocks, concrete, and other blockages crowded the roots, while the smaller trees were farther back, planted in rich soil that ran deep.

While the kids climbed on the uprooted roots of the big trees, the Lord said to me in His still and gentle voice, "Don't become top heavy, letting your own accomplishments and your status be the proof of intimacy with Me. Let your focus be on building faithful roots planted in the soil of My holiness and glory and not your own. This is the difference between those who are uprooted in the storms and who will stay planted and prosper."

The temptation in this world is to get bigger when we are truly called to get lower. Being top heavy means becoming concerned with our own glory and reputation. We feel the pull of being popular in the circles we hang out in, the desire to be known by our works and personality, the temptation to be egocentric and build little kingdoms we rule and thrive in. This is the desire of the enemy for our lives.

But God calls us to get low. He calls us to a life on our knees in repentance and devotion and into a deep relationship with Him. He asks us that we lay down our lives, our will, our kingdoms, our egos, and surrender it all to Him for His glory. He desires that we become devoted to Him alone, His will alone, His purposes and desires alone.

Do we want what we do for Christ to last? Of course we do. Do we want what we do in Christ's name to inspire and encourage others in their walk with the Lord? Yes! What we do and what we build will only last if God is the true source and foundation. Anything built outside of Jesus has a shelf life. Only what is done through the depths of surrender and relationship with God will last. As we think about our posture toward our purpose, we should strive to be deeply rooted trees with our priorities being what's below the surface rather than what's at the surface.

Becoming Deeply Rooted

Sadly, I'm sure we have all witnessed the public fall of spiritual giants. Men and women who have pursued their own kingdoms and popularity over the Lord's, causing them to become top heavy and planted in shallow soil. This isn't a new thing. People have been riding the wave of their God-given gifts and magnetic personalities in exchange for intimacy with God ever since the start of the human race. We just love being praised, being adored, and being seen by others. We have been misusing power, chasing personal gain and recognition, and praising our own talents and giftings over God's power and authority for generations. And time and time again, history has shown that when someone is elevated on charisma and gifting alone, they cannot withstand the weight of the responsibility handed to them. They become top heavy and shallow rooted.

Colossians 2:6-7 says, "So then, just as you received Christ Jesus as Lord, continue to live your lives in him, rooted and built up in him, strengthened in the faith as you were taught, and overflowing with thankfulness." Saying yes to Jesus as our Lord and Savior is not enough to carry us through the turbulence we will face as we pursue the calling He has over our lives. Hear me, it is not *just* believing, but it is becoming a devoted follower of Jesus. We must be forever students of His Word, continuing to live our lives in communion with Him as we abide in His presence. We must be women who choose to be rooted and built up in His way. We must be strengthened in the faith, not forgetting what we have seen and heard but always pressing further and further into His heart.

We want to be people who are thankful on all the sunny days and on the stormy ones. Not a toxic thankfulness that turns an eye away from pain and sorrow, but the thankfulness that comes from praising God for who He is no matter the circumstances we are facing. This is how we live deeply rooted lives. This is how we stand strong and sturdy in the middle of any attack or temptation from the enemy when we are going after the will and purpose of God.

We will all fall short of doing this perfectly. We are called to holiness and righteousness and God is looking for people who hold true repentance when they fall short. Repentance does not mean never messing up again, but it is the heart's desire to continue to follow after Jesus, pursue His way, and allow His grace and forgiveness to set us upright again. It is by grace alone, through Christ alone, that we can weather the storms and stand firm in the place that God is calling us to. A heart that is devoted and in a constant state of turning toward Jesus will be a heart that is deeply rooted in the pursuit of bringing glory to God. This is the soil that will last.

How do we become women who will not be uprooted in the storms? We've spoken about so many ways of abiding and following Jesus so far in this book, but I want to stress one more way that we grow deep and strong roots of faith: we become women who seek the presence of God. Being in the presence of God, specifically in prayer and worship, consistently and intentionally holds an atmosphere of transformation and power. It is in the presence of God that we are refined and our character is formed. Spending time praising God, listening to His Holy Spirit, and declaring His authority over our lives positions us to more accurately know and discern His will. And most importantly, spending time in God's presence brings Him honor and glory.

So you see, placing our devotion in Jesus nourishes the roots of our faith and by default what we build in Christ for the glory of His name and the good of others. And continually actively being in the presence of God to worship, praise, and listen to His voice purifies our hearts and sets us in alignment with His will and purpose. Think of time in His presence like the watering of the soil in which we are planted. It will cleanse, feed, and restore our hearts to His. Amen?

Nurturing Our Gifts

We know that being in God's presence and devoted to intimacy with Him places us in good soil to grow. But how do we know we are producing godliness in our lives, and what does godly character look like? Personalities and charisma will not sustain us to do what God has called us to do, and they will not equip us to stand firm in God when we are faced with temptation and trials.

We have made the mistake of elevating gifting over character time and time again. We see people who have a natural talent and a charismatic personality and immediately slap the "spiritual leader, pastor, small group leader" badge on them. I'm not just referring to other people—I'm talking about all of us. To qualify someone based on their gifting is a clear path to destruction unless we are nurturing that gifting with pillars of spiritual disciplines and accountability. Each of us, in whatever influence we are given by God, need to be more concerned with the quality and foundation of our character over our gifting and talent that God gave us for free.

I like to think of our natural giftings and talents as God's freebie way of guiding us into specific directions. He sometimes gives us the "natural talent" to set us on the right path, but natural talent was never meant to sustain us. Our natural talents and giftings are flawed until we align them and surrender them to become purified and holy through Christ. Are you following me? When we bring our talents and giftings to Christ, He alone purifies them and uses them for their holy and true purpose. This is the same with our character. Our personality and character are sanctified and made holy through the power of Jesus. When we know God and we allow Him to transform us we begin to take on the character of the Holy Spirit, who is alive and active within us.

What does a godly character look like? Remember when God reminded me not to compare my success based on outward appearance but on intimacy with Him? Instead of basing success on audience, popularity, or status, we can refer to God's standard. The fruit of the Spirit is evidence of our communion to God and our source of devotion.

> *But the fruit of the Spirit is love, joy, peace, longsuffering, kindness, goodness, faithfulness, gentleness, self-control. Against such there is no law. And those who are Christ's have crucified the flesh with its passions and desires. If we live in the Spirit, let us also walk in the Spirit. Let us not become conceited, provoking one another, envying one another (Galatians 5:22-26).*

The attributes listed above are the character and nature of God Himself. When we accept Christ and invite the Holy Spirit to dwell in us (as the temple itself) we will demonstrate these characteristics as a result of leaning into and being led by God's Spirit. A whole lot of the time my eyes hover over the gentleness and self-control part in Galatians 5:22-26 and I twitch a little. I do not do these things well. But you and I have the help and gentleness of the Holy Spirit to nudge us and teach us how to be more like Him.

We are all a showcase of God's diverse characteristics. On the spectrum of personality types we see people who wear their heart on their sleeves, whose presence is known the moment they step into a room. These women tell stories with so much confidence and charisma you can hear them a mile away. They celebrate in grandiose ways, motivate crowds, boulder through adversity, and are the first to raise their hand in class.

God bless the "first to raise their hand in class" people. What would us introverts do without them—am I right or am I right?

We know women who land on the other end of the spectrum where their tenderness and listening ears are their superpower. They work in mysterious ways behind the scenes, and they venture into the realm of intimacy easier than others.

All women, no matter their personality or stage of life, are reflections of a great and wonderful God.

There is certainly a place where we can hand off tasks and responsibilities based on personality tendencies and giftings... but to stop there is where we are at fault. Your personality type does not dictate your calling. Your score on personality tests does not decide where you should go and what you should do. While all these tools can certainly help you better understand yourself in relation to others, it is not a factor when it comes to the call God has placed on your life. Gosh, how we have boxed people in based on personality, status, who they know, where they come from, and what they wear.

The Lord does not look at the things people look at. People look at the outward appearance, but the Lord looks at the heart (1 Samuel 16:7).

It's right there, you guys. As plain and simple as that. We look at what our eyes can see, but God looks into the depths of our hearts and calls us from that place. He sees our potential and our destiny despite our outward qualifications. He is the one who puts us where we need to be planted and helps us stay firmly grounded in Him to sustain that position for His glory, our good, and the good of others. I love this about our God. In a world that is so quick to judge, so quick to dismiss and throw aside people who don't fit in, God calls the least of us to be part of His mission.

It's not a crime to want to dress nicely and trendy or to enjoy cute aesthetics and curated spaces. But these are all secondary and supporting roles to the main thing: Jesus, the first and highest thing that matters. To bear fruit that glorifies Him, we must look to the fruit of the Spirit to know how healthy the roots are. To sustain the position and platform the Lord calls us to, we must grow our character and intimacy with the Father.

Thrive Where You're Planted

A handful of women have inspired me to go and do the thing God has called me to do. Outside of my personal relationships I have been inspired by women I have seen speak at large conferences, women who are New York Times best-selling authors, and women who have won gold medals and Nobel prizes. These women are known by the masses all over the world for their work, and they have encouraged and inspired me to give my best yes to God. One of the common denominators these women have is that they are famous in their circles of influence. There is nothing wrong with the fact that they are famous and loved by so many. Their work has attracted so many eyeballs and God has used them in so many ways.

To be famous isn't "un-Christian." It is not inherently wrong to be widely known. God elevated David to king in the Old Testament, a king who was wise, famous, and loved by the people. The problem lies in finding purpose, validation, and our foundation in others' approval and praise. The problem is being concerned about the outward and uncensored about the unseen root system. The applause of man is fleeting and unstable and will ultimately leave us burned out and starving for a deeper fulfillment. Being known and loved by an audience isn't the same as being known in our real and vulnerable lives. When people admire us for something we *do* and we put all our joy and identity in that praise, we set ourselves up for a major letdown and disappointment.

Living for the next dose of approval and praise, like a dopamine hit, sends us into an unhealthy mental state. We all know how it feels when we get those likes and follows on social media. It gives us a boost we ride until we need the boost again. But living for the applause and approval of man is an empty well. When we set our hearts to digging deep roots in abiding in God and pursuing godliness through His Word we will learn to appreciate the applause of man but not live by its fuel.

We see in the Bible that the authors use the metaphor of trees to describe our spiritual stature. We know we are to be rooted in God, to be planted in good soil, and to bear godly fruit. God also gives us the analogy in a beautiful passage in Jeremiah 17:7-8 that describes what a person can look and be like when they are flourishing in their intimacy and calling.

> *But blessed is the one who trusts in the Lord, whose confidence is in him. They will be like a tree planted by the water that sends out its roots by the stream. It does not fear when heat comes; its leaves are always green. It has no worries in a year of drought and never fails to bear fruit.*

I don't know about you, but I want to be like that tree who trusts in the Lord, whose roots drink from the water of life. I want my leaves to always be green and alive no matter the season. I want to produce good and faithful fruit even in a season of drought. This path no doubt has nothing to do with charisma, talent, or the amount of eyeballs watching. It is solely based on the abiding and the fruit from the true source. The roots of faithfulness, obedience, love, and grace that hold tight no matter the weather. I want to be *that* tree.

Going where God is calling you will require you to have deep, strong roots in His Word. Your freebie gifts and talents alone will not be enough to get you to where He is calling you and certainly are not enough to sustain you in that place. Friend to friend, I urge you to press into intimacy with Jesus, desiring roots of godly character in your life. We need you to not uproot when storms come around. More than ever, we need grounded and unshakable, strong women who bless their lands and the people in them.

Rewind back to the start of this chapter, to the tornado I witnessed uproot the biggest trees in the field. Those big ol' trees—man, the way they fell down left so much destruction. All the birds that had built their little homes in their branches, just gone. The debris was spread out far and wide and the wind took all the loose limbs and rotted out branches and threw them into people's homes and cars. The damage was explosive.

And now picture those smaller, seemingly weaker and thinner trees behind the large ones, still standing strong, unmoved. They looked a little disheveled, but we won't judge them for that. Their roots were fully intact; they stood tall and upright when everything was destroyed around them. Their roots were planted in the good soil and the roots were deeper than they were tall. And ain't that the hope for each of us? How we are planted matters. Our lives will either bless others for generations or fall and leave a trail of destruction behind us.

You, my friend, have been made to weather the storms that come, and come they will. Your roots will be as strong as the fruitfulness of your calling if you plant them in good soil. Our world needs people who stand firm even when temptation comes calling.

Imagine us all, in a field of... I don't know, pick your tree—I'm choosing a magnolia—all planted together doing the good work put inside of us. And look, the storms come but they only water us because we grow in character through them. We've chosen the rich soil of godliness, and we have planted ourselves by the stream of living water. This is our destiny! First Timothy 4:8 tells us, "For physical training is of some value, but godliness has value for all things, holding promise for both the present life and the life to come."

Note: it says that physical training is of *some* value. I remind my husband of this when I don't want to lift weights with him. Put that in your back pocket for times when you can't be bothered with nonsense like exercise. But hear me, *godliness* has value for all things. Let's be women who are in pursuit of godliness, godly character, and a foundation deeply rooted in devotion to Jesus. In this space of flourishing, we will stand firm in the storms and produce fruit that lasts generations.

The Peace of Saying No

During the pandemic we were waiting on the Lord to fulfill the calling He had given us to move to Los Angeles. During that time, I would put on the YouTube videos from the sermons of the church I now attend in person in Glendale, California. The girls would play, and I would worship and most times cry with the worship team so many miles away, praying for breakthrough and open doors. We didn't have it in our own strength and resources to make the move on our own, and all I knew to do was press in with prayer and thanksgiving.

While living in Tulsa we were attending the church that raised me. It was a precious surprise to be in my church home again in the middle of so much unknown. Everyone knows me at my home church. I was raised there, did all the mission trips, attended every camp and youth event, and always lit the candles at the Epiphany service. I was a supported missionary from my church and poured back into the youth group as a twenty-something. I slept in the pews at overnight events, studied in the church library, and know all the good hiding spots.

One Sunday our missions director approached me about applying for a full-time job as the senior high women's youth pastor. My knee-jerk reaction was, "YES!" My youth pastors were and still are my superheroes, and the thought of being "them" to other teenagers was a huge honor. Josh and I talked about it and agreed I would fill out an application and see what happened. We didn't know what was going to happen with California, and as far as I could see no doors were opening for us to move.

The church staff had approached me, so I knew my chances of being officially offered the job were high. I filled out the thorough application, spent too much time finding the right interview outfit, and prepared with my husband what I would say in the interviews. First, I was interviewed by the two current youth pastors... it was a home run. Next, my one-on-one interview with our senior pastor... it went seamlessly. The eldership and pastors said I would hear from them soon... so I waited.

The job fit me like a glove. All the requirements for the job were in my wheelhouse of expertise. I'd felt called to ministry my whole life, I enjoyed discipleship work with this age group, it was within a church home that I knew and loved... and I got an office. I'd always wanted an office. On paper this was a no brainer, a quick and easy yes. Everyone I knew told me I was made for this job and that I would thrive. I had the support of my family and friends, and I knew I would do good, meaningful work within this context. Everything was feeling peachy until it wasn't.

A phrase God has always used to help me navigate His leading in life is to "follow His peace." If I could always stay true to following God's peace, then no matter what I faced I knew I was where I should be. The morning I received the call I knew in my spirit it wasn't meant for me. Excitement and willingness, those feelings were there. The added paycheck and personal office, not too bad. But the peace wasn't there. I knew I would need to turn down the job if it was officially offered to me.

The phone rang later that afternoon and I took the call on the front porch as the sun was shining on my face. He spent a few minutes telling me all the ways I was qualified for the job and how the whole staff and pastor were thrilled to have me on board. It would be a two-year minimum commitment, and I would start within a couple of months.

I kept checking my heart, and the peace was still not there. I knew it wasn't right.

"We want to officially offer you the position of youth pastor," he said.

I had no good reason to turn down the position other than to tell him the honest truth. That I was honored, humbled, and thankful for the opportunity and support, but I ultimately couldn't take the job because I wanted to walk in obedience, and God was asking me to say no.

When the phone call ended I looked up into the sun and the peace of God washed over me. I was joyful, content, and full of peace. I knew I'd made the right decision. In that moment I felt God's Spirit tell me, "Just because it's good doesn't mean it's right. Stay faithful to My calling in California."

Just because it's good doesn't mean it's right.

Those words have stuck like sticky tack to my heart. This worldview changes everything if we live by it. Posture your heart to know that just because it is good doesn't mean it's right for you.

Have you ever had to say no to something good so you could say yes to what was right? There is an infinite number of paths we can choose in this lifetime. Free will is a real thing, you guys. We have all been given talents and giftings and skill sets, a head full of dreams and ideas and goals. God has called us to follow His path, His perfect plan for our one glorious and beautiful life. He tells us to "stay the course of faith" to continue to follow the path He has set before us. When opportunities arise, we must seek God's guidance to determine if they are in His will for our lives. Where is the peace of God leading? The gold is found when we stay diligent in seeking His peace, keeping in step with His plan.

So many times we can get really tired and worn down in the waiting and in the process of our calling. It can be more challenging than we anticipated, more complex. We find there are roadblocks and detours we must take, and we are confused why someone didn't give us a fast pass through these challenges. It's in these moments that we can be tempted to switch lanes to a direction that looks smoother and faster. But keep the course, my friend.

Taking Inventory

I remember in the very early years of being a mom there was a battle inside of me to do more. The dream of being a mom *and* dreams of writing and being more hands-on in ministry were at odds with each other. It may be different for others, but God was clear with me that I was to be at home with the kids in their early years. He said no many times to other personal endeavors such as online seminary, starting a small business, and bigger writing plans. I was to say yes to being present at home and very few other things.

I will admit this was a challenge for me. What God was calling me to looked different than what some of my other friends were called to. I had to learn that the peace, joy, and grace of God were found in full when I surrendered all the things I wanted to say yes to and chose only what He asked me to be obedient to. In that lane, I thrived. Later on, God would begin opening the door to other steps of obedience. If I had chosen to try and do it all outside of God's will for that season of my life, I wouldn't have experienced the grace and joy that was planned for me.

Sometimes saying no to one thing is necessary to give your best yes to the right thing. And there are a whole bunch of things we are going to need to say no to. I mean, a lot. Why? Because balance is a unicorn. You're great, but you can't do it all. You just can't. No one can! Even the women who are running the world have nannies, house cleaners, and all kinds of help. No one, I repeat no one, is doing it all. We are humans with limited capacities, limited hours in a day, and limited mental and emotional stamina. God created us in a way that we would depend on Him to fulfill the callings and purposes He places on our lives. What God has entrusted you to steward well in this season of life is going to require the time, space, and energy to do it well.

What are the things you know God is calling you to put your time and energy into right now, the things He is calling you to say yes to in this season? Do you feel like you have the capacity to do those things well? Or are there things in your life you have said yes to that God has not asked you to do? What are the things you need to remove so you can create the space to really focus on what God has for you now?

When you look at the areas of your life—family, friendships, work, you fill in the blank—each of those don't deserve to hold equal value or weight. Some things are more important than others and hold more value to your time and day. The goal is not to achieve the balance of all things. There are parts of your life that should absolutely outweigh the importance, time, and energy of others. What we should be aiming for is asking God with discernment what areas of our life should be holding the most of our time and resources, because we are limited human beings. Say yes to the season He is calling you into and be brave to say no to what He is not calling you into. I promise, God's faithfulness is true, and every dream that is in the will of God will come around.

I'm sure you've thought of a few things as we've gone through saying yes and saying no. Let's make a list right now—a prayerful, discerning list—of four things God is urging you to say YES to in this season of your life. In the spirit of vulnerability and doing this thing with you, I'll share my list of yeses right now.

→ Be the full-time caregiver of my children.
→ Take on most domestic responsibilities until the up-coming school year.
→ Write this book.
→ Commit to a weekly picnic dinner with close friends.

Each of these things comes with the pouring out of my time, money, spiritual gifts, and intentional relationships. This is a small list, I know. But right now, this is it, you guys. These four things I can do with care, intention, and joy because I have heard God say, *These are the values and actions that matter most right now; steward these well.* I'm saying no to a whole lot. I'm in a place right now where I max out quickly emotionally and physically and I am prayerfully asking God for help staying in my lane in this season.

Now it's time for the no list. This one is a doozy, you guys. The temptation is to justify everything you're currently doing, and maybe there is a chance you already have eliminated things that are affecting your obedience. If so, rock on! But if not, this part is for you.

Write a list of things you are currently saying yes to that are soul sucking, time wasting, and are in the way of serving your yeses.

Some of the things on my "no" list:

→ Being the classroom mom
→ Joining PTA
→ Co-leading Girl Scouts
→ Volunteering in church nursery
→ Attending the moms' group that meets every Thursday morning

→   Recording a new season of my podcast
→   Starting the coffee business I began

The list continues to grow. And notice, all these things are *good* things. It's not like the list is full of bad, harmful, clearly terrible things. All these activities and commitments are holy, good, life-giving, and important roles and services in our world and communities. But we have not been asked to do it all and be all—we have been asked to be obedient to the path to which God leads us. Our aim should be on doing the next right thing, not all the things.

Surrender People Pleasing

We have a real beast out there that is going to try and get us to be the gal that says yes to everything and overextends herself. That beast is called people pleasing. The tendency to please people can really rob us of an abundant life. People pleasing demands we hand over our schedules, duties, boundaries, and mental health. It stunts our growth, limits our ability to live full lives of purpose, and sucks the joy out of us. Other names for people pleasing include *approval seeking, accommodating,* and *approval-hungry.*

It's the worst.

Up until two years ago I was a chronic people pleaser. I would volunteer for everything, say yes to hosting every baby shower, show up for friends at the detriment of my own family, just so I didn't disappoint people. I found so much of my own value in what I did for other people, and I was so uncomfortable when I felt like I had let someone down. I would rather be walked all over than say no to someone, and that was a real disservice to myself and my relationships. I was living in a constant state of unease and hurry, mostly due to the fact that I was taking on everyone else's plans for my life and not being faithful to my own. I was neglecting boundaries, clear communication, and my responsibilities within my own family unit. It wasn't a sustainable or healthy way to go through life, and I needed to surrender those habits to God to break the cycle.

Saying yes to everything also meant I never really did anything well. I was stretched too thin, too wide, and too deep. I was saying yes to what God was calling me to do but also taking on what everyone around me was asking me to do. What I learned with time, therapy, and the Holy Spirit is that saying no is healthy for our relationships with people and with God. Being busy and overworked, even with ministry or other good things, is not a badge of honor to wear. Seeking obedience, healthy capacity, and wisdom to know between good and right is the path worth taking.

You might have heard the common phrase, "If the devil cannot make us bad, he will make us busy." Ain't that the truth. Think about it. We are anxious and burned out people largely due to being overworked, never resting, and always striving for more and more to fulfill the ache inside. As Christians we fall into this trap just like the rest of the world. It's easier to spot when we are purposely running ourselves into the ground, but it's a sly tactic of the enemy to make us busy bees for the Lord. God is not asking us to be busy workers for His glory. He is asking us to be in a relationship first and foremost, and from that foundation we joyfully obey and follow His leading.

That leading sometimes contains seasons of greater capacity, and some look like saying yes to one thing and restoring our souls in rest. All are paths of obedience unto the Lord. The goal is not to be busy for the sake of being busy, but to be busy and hard at work doing the things God has asked us to do. What is good and right for others may not be good and right for you, and that's the way the cookie crumbles.

God's No Always Means a Better Yes

The other layer to this discipline of saying no is the trust that is required when God closes a door. I'm a firm believer that if God shuts a door, He is preserving us for something even better! I believe in a God who is after our very best and wants to see us thrive in the plans He has in store for us. When God is urging us to say no to a relationship, a job, a business endeavor, or a move, we can rest assured He is leading us to a better yes.

God's no is always leading us to wholeness and godliness. His no could lead to protection, or it could be a guiding to a better future, provision, or character building. His no is never out of a place of anger, hatred, or meanness. But it can sure feel a lot more like a *withholding* than a protecting or preserving sometimes. I'm no stranger to times of complete lack of understanding of why God didn't open a door that I was sure was good for me. And can I tell you what, there is no real good way around this process. It's a "got to get to the other side of the thing" type understanding. Oftentimes it takes hindsight to understand God's plan for us, and in some cases we never know on this side of heaven. This can be confusing and frustrating. I get it.

Here's what we should do when we face down a no from God: we bring our feelings to God and some close friends, let them out, and then go straight to the truth.

God is good.
God is faithful.
God has good plans for me.
God is just.
God isn't a bad guy.

God loves me.

And we press on until our knowledge catches up to our feelings. Not the other way around.

Sometimes we have to say no in order to hold on to a promise that God has given us, turning away from the temptation to go after something that will satisfy us in the moment, like the job offer I had from the church.

Two months after I said no to the job at the church God opened the doors only He could open and we found an apartment in Los Angeles. Saying yes to that job would have delayed His promise at least two years. I am so happy and thankful for the prompting of the Holy Spirit that keeps us on the right course.

Friend, don't underestimate the power of learning when to say no so you can give your best and highest yes to God. I promise you that following God's peace will never fail you. I promise that God is going to be faithful and good when He closes a door. We can build our whole life on that one truth. Learning to say no is going to serve you and your family and all your beloved people in the best way. You will be better for this one discipline. And guess what, you don't have to start strong with this one. You can ease into it, slowly building the muscle of setting healthy boundaries and taking more time to jump to a yes when asked. Be intentional, start with a few things, and see where that takes you.

You are not destined for a life of angst and burnout. You are made for flourishing and thriving. An obedient life and that God-dream of yours needs some room to move and grow, and it will depend on your small and big nos to create that space. Keep the course, give your big yeses to the right things, and give your nos without shame and guilt to what's left.

God's plan for how your purpose will unfold is something we can't know or force. When I think back to the list I made at fourteen for my life, I'm so thankful God asked me to surrender that plan to Him. He had something much better in store for me and I get to follow Him in that plan moment by moment, day by day.

PART 3: PACE

EMBRACING

GOD'S TIMING FOR

OUR PURPOSE

CHAPTER TEN

Spiritual Grit

L et me start with a disclaimer. Against all preconceived ideas you may have about me based on the fact that I cannot run a mile to save my life, I am telling the truth when I say I was once a pretty decent basketball and tennis player. I know, you would honestly never know it based on my now wide mama hips and inability to touch my toes. But sometimes, when you least expect it, you will catch glimpses of that long-past era in my catlike reflexes when someone throws something at me from across the room, or when I make a comment about the Kentucky State offense during March Madness.

Between the ages of twelve and seventeen my memories are built of 92 percent going to drill practice and tournaments and 8 percent boy drama. I lived and breathed the competition, and spent an equal amount of time in American Eagle skirts as I did in baggy gym shorts and high ponytails. Playing sports taught me a lot, but the two lessons I took along with me were the value of hard work and discipline.

At the end of a season athletes will begin what's called off-season training. Competitive athletes focus less on competing and more on functional movement and strength training in preparation for the next season. They do drills, hit the gym, and stick to a rigorous workout and practice schedule. While we show up on game day to watch and cheer them on, they have spent hundreds of hidden hours putting in the work to be their best.

Now, we may not be gearing up for Wimbledon, but we sure have our own big "game day" we should be preparing for. Our game days may look more like pastoring on Sunday morning, book launches, grand openings, and saying yes to a move or adoption. It's the moments and seasons when people bear witness to our giftings and callings poured out in a more public arena. But those moments, the moments that we anticipate and dream up, are only as impactful as our off-season.

I don't know about you, but I've seen a whole lot of folks out here showing up to their game day with no off-season training. We really think that our natural gifting paired with enough passion is all that's necessary to do the job. Natural gifting just gets us pointed in the right direction, friends, but it will not sustain us and take us to the depths of our calling and purpose that God has in mind for us.

I loved watching tennis growing up and still do. Unless you've been living under a rock you've probably heard of the name Serena Williams. Imagine if this ten-time world champion, back when she was six years old, wanted to be the best but just showed up to her state tournaments with a racket and no coaching. "But she loves the game!" That should be enough, right? Nope. Serena put in the hours of consistent drilling, training, and building those muscles that would sharpen her aim, and give her power in her shots and wisdom in strategy on game day.

Friends, no one can coast for long on talent and charisma alone. Maybe for a minute, but not for the long haul. So many of us are so focused on game day that we don't take the off-season seriously.

For the Christian girl, our off-season looks like daily reps of prayer, worship, and abiding with God. It looks like developing the spiritual fortitude of endurance, peace, grace, hope, and love. It looks like strengthening our muscles of humility, compassion, surrender, obedience, and faith.

In Hebrews 12:1 it says, "Let us run with perseverance the race marked out for us, fixing our eyes on Jesus, the pioneer and perfecter of faith." We have been called to run the race set before us, and sometimes that race will require us to walk at a slow pace, other seasons we may need to pick up the pace to a light jog, and in some we are called to full-on sprint. But we cannot expect to walk, jog, or sprint if we have not been hydrating and spiritually training for the race. The pace of the life Jesus calls us to does not align with hustle culture, striving, or the grind; God calls us to faithful perseverance and dedicated hard work that relies on His guidance and timing.

Spiritual Pace

Our obedience to Christ invites us to be active participants in not just believing in Jesus but becoming like Him as His disciple. Our faith is not lazy, and while we thrive in the grace God has given us, grace does not replace action. What I've noticed is that we have a tendency to swing from one extreme to another. I think we can easily do this when we talk about hustle and hard work. *Hustle*, the big bad word of the modern-day church. It had its moment, when we put *hustle* on water bottles and T-shirts.

But then we took the thing too far and hustle became our only strategy and we hustled our way to exhaustion and burnout. We ran and ran and ran without ever resting, jogging, or walking. We believed we just couldn't slow down or we would miss our shot. We hustled and didn't ever learn to rest. We began to sprint and we never trained, never drank from the well, and cramped up and had to be hauled off the track for a long recovery. Anyone else? Spiritual rest and grace were missing from the equation.

Our culture today used and abused hustle. We strived on our own strength, we pushed and pushed until burnout, and we ran our race without discipline. We relied on our hustle alone to achieve the God-dreams we have and found ourselves exhausted. As an attempt to course correct from the hustle fatigue, we went all the way to the opposite side and fell into patterns of being lazy and stagnant, and slapping words like *rest* and *grace* over it.

There are seasons of walking, jogging, running, and sprinting. But no matter which phase you are in, giving your all and conditioning for your mission are going to keep you moving forward. In Philippians, Paul says,

> *Whatever you do [whatever your task may be], work from the soul [that is, put in your very best effort], as [something done] for the Lord and not for men, knowing [with all certainty] that it is from the Lord [not from men] that you will receive the inheritance which is your [greatest] reward. It is the Lord Christ whom you [actually] serve (Philippians 3:14, AMP).*

Whatever your task may be, work from the soul and put in your very best effort! And as you work hard and give it your best effort, surrender the outcome to our sovereign God, and rest in His peace and grace to sustain you on the race set before you.

As you work hard, God's promise is that His presence will go with you and give you rest. Just like He gives His comfort, peace, and joy through His Holy Spirit, His rest, refreshment, and renewal will be at your side. If we are running on the path He has given us, if we are saying yes in obedience to His steps and purposes, His rest is with us.

And He said, "My presence will go with you, and I will give you rest" (Exodus 33:14).

Not only will He give us His continual rest, but He will show us how to maintain good health and boundaries through rest. Psalm 23 tells us He will lead us beside still waters and make us lay down to rest. Our path, friends, is along renewing waters. We have all we need along the way. But it's both, right? It's hard work and rest, playing their part in holy tandem. All these things coincide and are meant to serve us well.

In fact, I personally know a lot of women who hustle hard on their God-given mission all while leaning into surrendered obedience and submission to God's grace, ability, and power. They work their spiritual muscles daily, abiding, worshiping, and praying to God. When God says pick up the pace, they do it, and when God says take the bench and rest, they do it. When God says hustle to the finish line, they sure do it. Women of God are not lazy—they take their mission seriously and complete it with vigor!

Do you see how hard work and rest go hand and hand? We do not choose one and run with it. We do not only hustle and burn out or rest and become lazy. We choose the redemptive purpose of hustle, which is hard work and endurance, and we also choose spiritual rest and grace. They are to work together, giving us a strong foundation to run our race.

Burnout and spiritual lethargy is not our portion. Amen?

What a Gritty Woman Looks Like

When we talk about women who work hard and rest well do you have someone who comes to mind? These women are gold, right? The kind we look up to and want to be like. I call these women, women with that holy grit. They have that grit that produces perseverance and long obedience that I admire so much. They are not weak damsels-in-distress women. They are strong, confident, and gritty in their faith because they are secure in who they are and in a deep connection with God.

What a gritty woman looks like:

→ She is bold, strong, and resilient.
→ She is steadfast and courageous, full of perseverance and character.
→ She is full of grace and humility, in submission to Jesus, the One who supplies all she needs.
→ She is not reliant on her own strength and ability, but on God's.
→ She is hardworking and diligent in all she does.
→ She believes in the promises and faithfulness of God, despite her circumstances.
→ She is daring, loving, and unafraid of failure.
→ Her life belongs to God.

Gritty women press on, work hard, rest well, and stay faithful in perseverance. This life of deep and meaningful soul work that brings about holy grit is one that produces that good and long-lasting fruit we want. It's what legacy is made of and is the foundation to a meaningful and purposeful life. Do you want to be known as a woman of grit? I sure do! And I want that kind of life and character for every one of us.

Do you remember when the first *Lord of the Rings* movie came out? It was released in 2001, which was about, let's say, one million years ago? I went to the midnight showing like young people did and watched this incredible three-hour movie. There is this memorable scene when Arwen, a half-elven young woman, is being chased by seven dark horses with riders that look like grim reapers. They form a "v" shape around her, closing in. She rides harder, not breaking her gaze in front of her. She is galloping as fast as she can through open land, steadfast, determined, and fixed on her destiny. It wasn't so much about how fast she was riding that sent goosebumps down my arms, but it was the unseen strength, courage, and fearlessness in her eyes. She had something else within her that was stronger and bigger than the evil that was after her.

I sat in my sweaty theater seat with watery eyes watching her. *That! Whatever she has, I want it. I want to be like that.*

We want the inner strength that proves itself powerful in times of immense trial and failure. We want to be the kind of woman who is fixed on Jesus, brave, bold, and determined. The kind of woman who is not shaken by the evil that is out to destroy us but is instead steadfast and anchored to a victorious God. We don't want to just be fast and successful. We want to carry a hidden strength and perseverance that goes beyond what any self-help book or motivational speech could offer us. We want the real thing. We want to say yes to God and yes to the assignments He has given us and go after them with some fierce holy grit.

> *Therefore, since we have been justified through faith, we have peace with God through our Lord Jesus Christ, through whom we have gained access by faith into this grace in which we now stand. And we boast in the hope of the glory of God. Not only so, but we also glory in our sufferings, because we know that suffering produces perseverance; perseverance, character; and character, hope. And hope does not put us to shame, because God's love has been poured out into our hearts through the Holy Spirit, who has been given to us (Romans 5:1-5).*

A sign of holy grit is the ability to persevere when things get really hard. It's the decision you make in your heart that you are going to do this life and go after this thing God's way. When easy routes come up, when placing all control back into your own hands seems tempting, when you look foolish and crazy, your decision to stand firm and hold on to God's promises will release the breakthrough. Grit is not allowing our own perspectives and our own ability to get in the way of God's supernatural ability, provision, and leadership in our lives. Your holy grit will take you further and higher than hustle ever could. Grit takes perseverance with Jesus and daily making the choice to do this life with Him.

Perseverance and a committed life with Jesus will bear good, kingdom fruit not only in our lives but for the generations to come. If that doesn't get you excited to walk with Jesus then read that again! Your commitment to follow Jesus and do things His way will bless you and the generations after you. That means that what you do today and tomorrow doesn't end when you die, it blesses your kids and their kids and their kids' kids. That's a road worth choosing.

What Scripture says we gain through the challenges we face is the ability to persevere. *Perseverance* is the key word to describe people who are people of grit. Grit is a way of saying, "That girl is persevering through hardship. That girl is steadfast in the direction she is set on. That girl isn't surviving, she's thriving, even in the suffering."

This perseverance will reward us with more than just goals met or boxes checked on our to-do list. This holy perseverance will build in us godly character that will bring fruition in our lives. And at that place of maturity we replace our fears and doubts with hope. Hope in a God who promises eternal good to those who will deny themselves and walk in obedience toward Him.

I see women who are living from a place of grace and grit all around me. Every day, seemingly normal women are becoming spiritual giants by their decision to live obedient lives to God and stick it out with Jesus.

These women, you, and me, we are invited into so much more than a popularity contest or the road to quick success. We have the opportunity to live in the abundance of God, to become the women of grit we are all called to become. We have the choice to choose between the way of perseverance and surrender, or the path of control and hustle. We will reap and produce the fruit of the path we choose to take.

Meet Me in the Off-season

Jim Elliot said, "Wherever you are, be all there! Live to the hilt every situation you believe to be the will of God."[2] Whether we are in seasons where we feel we are meeting the true potential of our God-given purpose, or we are in the off-season, where we feel like we are working hard without much to show for it, we should live wholeheartedly for God.

The off-season may just feel, well, off. But God brings off-seasons into our lives for a reason. These seasons don't mean God has abandoned us or we aren't taking any steps closer to our assignment. In fact, they often mean we are in the midst of working out our assignment with God. God uses seasons of downtime and hard work to prepare us for seasons when we are in the spotlight. It is through the off-season that He helps us develop the character we need to represent Him well when we are fulfilling His purpose for our lives in more evident and more public ways.

Are we called to work hard? Yes. Will we encounter challenges, seasons that require more sprinting than others? Yes. Hard work on God's path and for His glory will bear peace, joy, and a sense of great accomplishment. Spiritual rest from a pace of obedience to God's race set before us will look like His peace forever with us, His power and strength filling us, and seasons of resting by His renewing waters.

2   Elliot, *The Journals of Jim Elliot,* 172.

We are called to be women with powerful grit! So I am here to encourage you today to do the work and give it your all. I want to see you on your game days showing up ready and prepared in the Lord to do the task He has called you to do. And I want to encourage you to meet me in the off-season, building your spiritual disciplines of abiding, surrender, and obedience. Strengthen your muscles of prayer, worship, and community. And lean into the Holy Spirit to develop the perseverance, hope, and character that will sustain you for the long run.

Camping

There's a great camping site in Oklahoma called Greenleaf. Growing up, my parents would load up our van with camping gear and a big cooler of hot dogs and sodas, and we would spend some of my best childhood memories at this campground. For the record, this wasn't intense camping. Just in case you have any misconceptions about the severity of survival of this campground, let me set the scene. There were full bathrooms and showers. Paved walkways, mile-long hiking (no incline) that was marked with a red spray paint on the sides of trees. Each camping spot was also marked and had a man-made fire pit ready for s'mores.

Oh, and there was a miniature golf course.

At Greenleaf, I felt like an explorer. I would trek the hiking trail pretending to be discovering new land, looking out for bears and other wild things hiding in the trees and marveling over every speckled rock or large fallen leaf. As a wide-eyed six-year-old I loved the way the leaves of the trees would sway back and forth above me, and the sound of small animals skipping off as we approached them. I was always sure to find a tall and skinny walking stick to fully embrace the outdoor experience. The hiking trail at Greenleaf leads to a wooden, rickety bridge I always felt particularly proud of myself for crossing. Like I said, the trail was short and worn and the bridge was hardly dangerous but I didn't see it that way. Little me was experiencing challenges, overcoming fears, and learning new skills every time we camped. To me, Greenleaf was the ultimate nature experience, and nothing could top it.

Until I got a bit older.

I was a young mom to our firstborn, Cora, who was a bouncy two-year-old at the time. We packed our bags and headed north to go camping with Josh's family in the Boundary Waters, which is in northern Minnesota. As we drove miles and miles into the woods I was wide-eyed again. I had never seen nature like this. So untouched, so quiet and serene. Trees so tall and strong I felt vulnerable and small but in the best kind of way. I thought, *This must be what Eden was like. A place that held surreal peace and wonder.*

We spent the first night in a small cabin near the water and woke up with the sun early the next morning to begin our portage. It was chilly outside and a layer of dew covered the ground. The fog hovering over the lake looked like ghosts but in a beautiful, non-creepy sort of way. We ate breakfast, threw back some coffee, packed up, loaded the canoes, and off we went.

I'm proud to say we started strong. It wasn't until the first stop that I realized what portaging actually meant. To portage is to canoe for a distance and then unload said canoes, carrying them through a trail that leads to another lake—are you sweating yet? You have to haul personal belongings down the trail as well, then repack the canoe and on you go until you come to the next portage. No one told me that having strong calves and anything resembling core strength was needed for this excursion. And don't forget, we took our two-year-old on this trip—you know, like normal people do.

Every mile deeper into the Great Lakes felt more and more otherworldly. The water sparkled and the trees were dark green and towering over us. Not an airplane in the sky. I remember canoeing through one of the lakes that day as Cora lay in her life jacket at the bottom of the canoe, napping. *Yes, girl, you feel it, too, don't you? That serene peace and wonder.* We smelled like sweat and mud by the end of the day, but it was totally worth all the hard work. Actually, the sweat and lower back pain made setting up camp even more sweet. We set up camp next to the water and stayed warm by a fire that night. I looked up at the stars and thought about how far away I was from that marked camping spot in Oklahoma.

I can't describe the beauty of the calm water, the peacefulness of the uninterrupted sounds of nature, and the connection I felt with God under the starry sky. It was like experiencing the world the way it was supposed to be. I was miles and miles away from my little childhood camping ground, where I first fell in love with the outdoors. Thinking back on being six years old at that little campsite, I would never have guessed there was something even bigger and more beautiful out there.

Today, right now, I'm not in the woods camping near a peaceful river, warming my hands by a crackling fire. I'm at my kitchen table with my cold coffee and bruised apples in the centerpiece bowl. Reminiscing, I'm considering what my perspective on camping would be if I had never ventured beyond Greenleaf. Greenleaf was my introduction to camping, the place where I learned to be brave and felt challenged, but in a more comfortable and secure environment. It was training for the bigger stuff I would experience later on in life.

The question I'm asking myself today and that I want to extend to you is this: Where have you set up camp? As we venture deeper into relationship with God, and as we step further into the purpose He has called us to, we need to move from our paved and comfortable camping grounds to a more challenging, uncomfortable, and uncharted path. To experience the fullness of what God has for us and to move on to the next thing He is calling you toward, you will need to get out of your comfort zone.

There is no way around this step. The place you have been all this time has served you well, taught you what you needed to learn, and was good for a season, but sometimes we outgrow our space and God calls us onward. Now is the time to go to uncharted territory, an invitation to greater relationship with God and greater wonder. Saying yes to the assignment means it's time to pack up camp, head north, and follow God's pace for your journey.

Step Out of the Boat

In Matthew 14 we find a classic felt-board Bible story of Jesus walking on water. As Jesus so nonchalantly walked on the water toward the boat where His disciples were, He invited Peter to join Him. At first all the guys thought Jesus was a ghost; I probably would, too, if I were there. They soon realized they were witnessing a real-life miracle. Peter at first was full of faith as he stepped out onto the water. He started off feeling good about the whole thing, trusting Jesus and leaving the comfort and security of the boat. Then, whoosh! Doubt came in and he lost sight of Jesus. I think it is safe to say Peter was outside his comfort zone. Never have I ever walked on water nor do I think I would have had an ounce of chill about it. Peter's doubt caused him to fall into the water, and as Jesus pulled him up He said to him, "Peter, why do you doubt?"

Peter shows us that as much as obedience takes faith, it also takes our willingness to take an uncomfortable step in order to deepen our relationship with Christ. The journey of following Jesus and moving in obedience to what He has called us to requires that we are OK with getting uncomfortable and choosing to fully trust God in choppy waters.

The cost of admission to an obedient and abundant life with Jesus is your comfort. As we choose the road of saying yes to obedience to Jesus and therefore choosing to follow His path, His way, and at His pace, you will be asked to leave your hypothetical, comfortable, low-risk camping spot. I'm here at this table with my bruised apples and cold coffee to tell you that the campground you have been living in has served you long enough. God allows us seasons of growing and learning, and then He calls us out of that territory and into a new one, continuing to grow deeper and wider until we outgrow that one. You were never meant to stay stagnant where you began. Discomfort, despite our human nature, isn't always a sign to retreat—it's an invitation to grow.

Be prepared—your human body will have all kinds of big feelings about this. Most people do not willingly and gracefully embrace discomfort. This is something I struggle with most days of my life. Sometimes we will go into the unknown joyfully with arms wide open, other times we will be shaky and hesitant. Our human nature tells us to run from the uncomfortable. It tells us to stay safe, stay still, stay where we are, stay in control, and be unsurprised.

Honestly, we should be thanking our bodies for the way they protect and nurture us. God gave us bodies that can heal themselves, restore DNA, and create life, for crying out loud. But again, there is a big difference between listening to our body's natural protective mechanism and spiritually releasing control over to the Holy Spirit. Releasing control over to God to do the necessary pruning and growing in our lives is what we are talking about here.

No one is saying to get out of your comfort zone by tossing away logic and wisdom and putting yourself in physical danger for the sake of "getting uncomfortable." No. We are saying yes to getting out of our comfort zones by releasing control over the discomfort that comes with spiritual growth and moving on toward what God has called us to do. In our spiritual sanctification we will undergo seasons of pruning. In the same way a tree must be cut back to then grow and produce more flourishing, Jesus prunes away parts of us so that we can enter into a new season of growth. What looks like going backward is really moving forward.

Sometimes God calls us into new territory that looks like:

→ Saying yes to a new job
→ Saying yes to a big move
→ Saying yes to a course of education
→ Saying yes to writing that book
→ Saying yes to speaking in front of crowds
→ Saying yes to starting that small group

Whatever your next yes is, it's OK to be shaking in your boots about it. Being scared and uncomfortable when doing something you know God has assigned for you is 100 percent normal. You can do it scared. You can do it with sweaty pits and palms. You can be full of butterflies and still say yes.

Good Enough Isn't Your Promise

As we journey on with God, every new level of growth will mean a new level of discomfort and release of control. The temptation to clench our fists and hold tight to any control can only grow roots of fear, anxiety, and burnout. Being uncomfortable in order to grow and accomplish what the Lord has set before us is a feeling we will learn to see as a necessary step of the process.

To hold on to our comfortability is just another way of being sure we stay in control. We want our little fingers on everything.

We place tangible things as our form of comfort to keep us grounded. We rely on our means of control to ensure we never fail, get hurt, or rock the boat. We put so much effort toward creating a comfortable life that we never leave the campground we began in and forfeit the beauty of connection Jesus invites us to. Not only the relationship with the Father, but the assignment He has for us as well.

I want you to know that God desires for you to release the tight grip you have on control and choose to trust in Him in the atmosphere of His presence. In the presence of God is where we can find true comfort, not the counterfeit version we create for ourselves. God wants this so much that when He sent the Holy Spirit He called Him the Comforter. The Holy Spirit is God within us all the time, supplying all that we need. Like Peter, as we step out of our comfort zone and into what feels like unsteady ground, we carry permanent comfort through the Holy Spirit. Our comfort is found in the depths of our relationship with Him, not in our circumstances. There is more to see and experience with Jesus if we would only venture on with Him.

I can't get my friend's simple text out of my head: *"Don't camp outside your Promised Land. Good enough isn't your promise."*

Just when I started digging roots in a place of false security and comfort she's the one to kick me in the butt and remind me to keep going toward Jesus. Her text reminded me, and I hope it reminds you, too, that settling for "good enough" in your life is not your inheritance.

Good enough is sandwiched between your no to God and your yes to God. The good-enough zone is the place where we want to go all in with God but we allow fear, discomfort, and doubt to get the better of us and decide to go half way. We tell ourselves, "Well, at least I didn't say *no*." So instead we become complacent. We love this good-enough zone because life is neutral here. We feel like we have things under our control, nothing is rocking our boat or shaking us up, just the way we like it. We feel good here because all the control is in our hands and we can picture the outcome. No surprises. We protect ourselves from failure by never fully going all in.

I might not know you in person, but I'm willing to bet that if you picked up this book you have a desire and passion in your heart, given by God, that He is asking you to walk bravely toward. Hear me when I say your obedience will never be without a cost. Jesus has paid the price for our salvation, and our allegiance to a life with Him will require our surrender. The cost is our willingness to release our strong grip over the areas we have held so tightly in our control.

Our inheritance is not to be destitute; our inheritance is actually flowing with goodness, the abundance of joy and peace and the fruit of living with the Holy Spirit. You are destined to live in the land promised to you, one where your assignment and gifting can thrive and multiply for the good of God.

The Israelites, a people God freed out of slavery in Egypt, were called to a land promised by God, set aside for their flourishing and good. Instead, the Israelites disobeyed God and wandered in a desert only a few miles from where they had been called to thrive. They set up camp in a place of good enough and in disobedience worshiped other gods, formed their own vices for comfort, and wandered around for forty years.

They didn't miss out on the Promised Land because they were bad at directions but because they were disobedient to God. Let's talk about this. In the moment between their deliverance and their promise, they chose to worship idols and turn from God. They lacked faith in the God who called them out, and that lack of faith and fear led them into disobedience. They decided they would take the reins and create their own way, their own god, and their own resources.

Shoot, we do this. If the Israelites, who were slaves God supernaturally delivered through crazy plagues and wild miracles—like, I don't know, parting an entire sea in half—can allow the fear of not being in control and not having faith in God take over, then can't we all?

I don't know about you, but I don't want to be a wanderer. I want to actively choose to obey God when it comes to my life and all that comes with it. I want to step boldly into the land promised and destined for me, and lead my children and the next generation into the land God has for them, too.

Here's the thing—the only one who can get you to your Promised Land is the one who brought you out of your mess and led you through the wilderness in the first place. The Promise Maker is the Promise Giver. There's no entering the fullness of the assignment He gave you without Him being the leader. Oftentimes in the middle of the *present* and the *promise* we get tired of waiting. We get uncomfortable and we want to take matters into our own hands, but this is not the Jesus way. We are called to stand firm, abide, surrender, hear, and obey.

God Provides What You Need

Stepping toward your Promised Land full of the assignments God is asking of you will require that you step out of your comfort and control. Sometimes that will look like letting go of what you know, what's comfortable, predictable, and good enough.

When we are living in the tension between where we are now and where we are being called to go, we can easily look ahead at that unknown place and frankly just prefer to stay put... especially when where we are is the good-enough option. We have the choice to choose good over best. But like I said, good enough isn't your inheritance. The comfort we are choosing over the unknown, wild, brave, obedient walk with Jesus can seem perfectly fine. It will be tempting to want to stay in the place you know, where you have a grip on the outcomes of your efforts. It will be tempting to look around at where you are without the ability to fully see what's ahead and want to say no to the path. I say, go scared and wobbling in the direction God is bringing you.

Don't settle.

Don't give into the trick of false comfort.

Don't believe the lie that God's best for you couldn't really be better than what you would have to surrender.

Don't say no.

Don't say yes but only this far.

Say yes. All in.

This journey isn't without suffering. That's a given. But if suffering is part of life then I would much rather suffer in a way that produces perseverance, character, and hope—saying yes to Jesus, stepping out of the boat—over suffering in a place of false securities that leads to stagnant faith. If I must face trials, I want to face them with purpose. I want the hard stuff of life to propel me toward Jesus and make me more like Him, growing in holiness and closeness toward our Heavenly Father.

> *Not only that, but we rejoice in our sufferings, knowing that suffering produces endurance, and endurance produces character, and character produces hope, and hope does not put us to shame, because God's love has been poured into our hearts through the Holy Spirit who has been given to us (Romans 5:3-5, ESV).*

We know that saying yes will be hard. And we know that saying yes and walking in obedience isn't always going to mean that all the people we love and places we love will go with us. But our sight is limited, and our ability to comprehend the good things God has prepared for us is flawed. So we must trust that when He's calling us onward into the unknown, He is already there, and He will be our comfort, our home, our peace and joy. He's the only true and lasting source of it.

His promise is this: He will be with us until the end of the age. His comfort, peace, and joy will be with you until the end. You can trust Him at His word.

Don't settle and pitch your tent outside of God's best for you. I promise, looking back you will see that the easy trail and lit campsite you find comforting and safe doesn't compare to the starry sky and healing waters of where He is taking you. Pack up camp, get off the boat, and do what you gotta do, because the True Comforter is beckoning you to follow Him onward.

Waiting Well

On December 31, 2014, Josh and I, along with our eight-month-old baby, Cora, moved out of our little chalet in Burtigny, Switzerland, to the bustling city central of Amsterdam. We had served just under a year in Switzerland as full-time volunteers with a Christian organization, and we felt like we were to staff a school at a sister base in Amsterdam.

Amsterdam was dark and cold when we arrived. We were driven to our new home for the next three months, which was an old four-story building called Samaritan's Inn. A warm and inviting coffee shop, *Dwaze Zaken* ("foolish things" in Dutch), occupied the bottom floor, and at the top of the building in big blue letters read from one end to the other, *Jesus Loves You.* If you ever find yourself in Amsterdam just glance a little to the left when you step out of Centraal Station and you can't miss it. I suggest ordering the *dwaze latte* from the coffee shop—you can thank me later.

We shared a floor with several other people, all differing in ages and ethnicities. We had a common living space, shared a girl's and boy's toilet, cooked shoulder to shoulder in a small kitchen together, and divided up fridge shelving for food storage. We had one room to ourselves that had a loft bed and a wall full of windows that would later serve as a great people watching spot. I loved it there. Amsterdam is cozy in every sense of the word, and I'm all about cozy.

We staffed a discipleship training school for three months, and then led the students on an outreach to serve local churches and do ministry work in the Dominican Republic for three months. Cora turned one in Santo Domingo, and we celebrated her along with the students who became more like our family. When we got back, we were invited to stay on staff full-time with the Amsterdam base. We said yes!

Because of things like visas, finances, licenses, and a long list of documents needed, we headed back to Oklahoma to get all the necessary paperwork in order. Things were flowing, and we couldn't wait to get back to the work we were a part of in Europe. But lo and behold something began to stir inside me and I couldn't make sense of it.

It happened slowly and uneventfully. I started thinking about the city of Los Angeles, had a couple random dreams about it, and then it became impossible to ignore. It was pulling at my gut and I couldn't shake it. I kept thinking, *What on earth is going on?* I couldn't tell if it was a stirring from God or something else. It wasn't, *How fun would it be to visit LA?* It was, *Oh, I think we really need to check out LA.*

I was in full panic. Things were going so well, we were quite literally packing our bags to move to Amsterdam, and I was about to ask if we could check out Los Angeles off of a gut feeling. But I knew it was more than just a feeling. I wasn't sure what it was, but I knew it was important. How incredibly inconvenient and weird of me to bring this up. This was no time for frolicking and being high maintenance, but here I was. I pulled Josh into my parents' room and blurted it out like a lunatic. "Listen, I know the reality is that we are packing our bags, signing visa paperwork, and have bought tickets and have given people our word that we are moving to Amsterdam . . . but there is something in me that's saying, go to LA. So can we go?"

We agreed we should not ignore whatever God was saying and before making the big transition to Amsterdam we should check it out. Rule it out? We bought tickets, left Cora with my parents, and flew to California for the weekend. My brother had been living in LA for a while by then so we crashed at his place and he gave us a tour of the city. I'm from the Midwest, and a whole lot of people there don't like the idea of the West Coast. But the moment we touched down at LAX I felt at home.

Since we had little to no idea what we were actually there to explore, we made our best guess and went to visit the volunteer base we would be working with in Amsterdam that was also in LA. It just made sense, and we figured that if we were to move to LA we would obviously be in a mission setting.

It was a total dud. The organization was great, the people were awesome, and they were doing work in the city that was admirable, but nothing clicked. I was super confused. Did I hear wrong? Was this a complete mistake? Those few days only increased my love for the city but made the whole idea of living there more confusing.

Have you ever experienced a time of feeling like God is saying something but it's just not quite lining up? Sometimes God will give us a dose of a calling, but the timing isn't right. It feels like He is hanging this idea of something we can't have out in front of us, but that's not His heart. Following God's pace/timing sometimes requires seasons of waiting. God will often give us seeds of promises that aren't ready to be fulfilled. When we wait well, we experience the fullness of His blessing.

The process of cultivating dreams into reality takes planting and preparing. That day in California the dream was planted, but it would take years of planning, growing, and preparing for that dream to reach maturity. Rushing it, pulling it up before there were any roots to sturdy the foundation would have been short-cutting the full promise. I didn't want it until God said yes, but for now He was saying, "Put it on the shelf and wait for My go."

Put It on the Spiritual Shelf

Let me tell you about this "shelf." The "shelf" is an imaginary thing Josh and I made up. I'm sure other people have their version of "the shelf" as well. The shelf is where we place things we don't understand or prayers that haven't been answered for a later time. We are not about shoving feelings down, throwing dreams in the trash, or allowing the unanswered questions and prayers to run wild in our minds and spirits. The shelf is our response to things we don't understand, promises we haven't seen come true, and dreams from God that need a bit more shelf life before taking them down. I'm telling you, the shelf is a game changer. The shelf is where things go to live, not die. Putting something on our spiritual shelf is a way we can be present in our journey today without dismissing something good God will do in the future.

The shelf requires us to trust God's timing and wait well. Waiting on the timing and promises of God can be challenging and stretching. Waiting is hard, waiting is inconvenient, waiting is a spiritual discipline most of us need to learn to do well. Learning to wait well and be present in the moment will help us not look back and wish we had been more present in the fleeting seasons.

If we force the promises God has for us instead of trusting Him with His timing and outcome, we can't pick up the things He is asking us to be faithful to today.

Every year I get older; it's wild. Time used to crawl by, but it's rushing by like a river after a storm these days. When my kids' birthdays roll around I am reminded of how quickly this time goes. In the beginning as a first-time mom the days would move so slowly. As much as I loved the time when the kids were small, I felt myself just wanting them to get to that next milestone faster. Some days I was so ready for them to be just a little more independent and for me to have a little bit more of my space back. Now I look back and wonder who came and sped up the clock. Can we slow it down? I haven't had shoulder pain from carrying a diaper bag or had to lug a stroller around in a few years. Time doesn't stop for any of us, and the seasons will pass like sand in our hands.

Don't let your excitement and desire for a dream God has given you steal the present moment. That dream is good and holy and will be absolutely incredible… when the time is right. In the meantime, start by thanking God for it, and think about it with joyful anticipation, not reckless worry and control. Allow God to say when that dream is ready to come off the shelf, because His timing will always be best. Easier said than done, right? I get it. I've been frustrated with God's timing countless times. But what I have to my advantage now is, well, time. Enough things that I placed on the shelf have now seen the light of day. I've gained the perspective to see how and when God chose to bring that dream into reality and how faithful He has been to do so. Not only that, but time has allowed me the good grace to fully see that His timing beats mine every time.

After we placed California and all the unknowns of that dream on our imaginary shelf, Josh and I took it down again and brought it to the Lord after we had completed our first two-year commitment in Amsterdam and had to decide to move on or re-up our commitment to the base. We sat together and asked God about it again. But it wasn't time, and the Lord said not yet. So we put it back on the shelf and continued faithfully where He had us.

Full transparency, there were many times I would cry and be angry about putting California back on the shelf. Waiting can be so disappointing and confusing. If you're holding a dream right now that you know is from the Lord but He is asking you to put it on the shelf and trust Him with the timing, I want to say that

I see you. It's no small thing to feel the ache of something you're passionate about being just out of reach. But we must remember that God is faithful to fulfill His promises and plans for us. He is trustworthy and good and desires to see us flourish on the path He has set for us.

Be Present with What's in Front of You

Let this verse be an encouragement to you today:

> *But those who hope in the Lord*
> *will renew their strength.*
> *They will soar on wings like eagles;*
> *they will run and not grow weary,*
> *they will walk and not be faint (Isaiah 40:31).*

Remember, we are going about this dream-chasing thing in a new and better way, and that means we are choosing to submit the timing and fruition of those dreams to our good God. On this path we can live out what Isaiah is talking about. We can wait on the Lord and be renewed—how about that? We can run this race before us at God's pace and not grow weary. Yes and amen! We will not grow faint and tired in our waiting because He has the capacity to sustain us. I'll take it. This waiting doesn't have to be the thing that sucks the life out of us, but rather a moment where we can remember to be present and alive with the assignment in front of us today. There are always people to love and to serve and ways to utilize the gifts you have; go do those things well and leave the rest on the shelf for later.

We are not the first people walking this earth who have had to learn to wait well. Let's name a few, shall we? First up, my personal favorite: Sarah, the wife of Abraham. This woman has been called the Mother of Nations because she waited on the Lord to give her children who God said would be as numerous as the sand on the shore. The stories of women who waited on the Lord to fulfill their promise of children are many. Rachel, Hannah, Elizabeth, Rebekah, and the mother of Samson were all waiting on the Lord. All these women had barren wombs but were carrying a promise. Then we have Mary, the mother of Jesus, who waited on the promise to bring forth a baby who would be the Messiah. What a group of strong and faithful women to have gone before us and set such a remarkable example of what waiting well looks like. They prayed, worshiped, dwelled in the temple of the Lord, and had joyful hearts that were full of hope for God to do what He said He would do.

Then there was David, who waited fifteen years before he became king. Joseph waited on the Lord in prison until God brought him out of slavery and into power. Job waited through suffering, believing that even in his circumstances God would redeem him. Daniel prayerfully waited on the Lord for a breakthrough and God heard his prayers.

The men and women who have led the way for us are people who are marked by strength in waiting. They have shown us that waiting on God is so worth it. Their examples tell us that when we wait on the Lord instead of forcing our timing and our way in our circumstances, God can bring so much fruit from our lives. When God asks us to wait on Him this is not a sign of His rejection. Waiting on Him allows the best possible outcome and the fullness of the promise to take place. Waiting gives space for abundance where our impatience squashes it.

Our greatest example in waiting is found in Jesus Christ. He waited well as He was living on a mission to do the Father's will. Being fully God and fully man He had the power to summon angels, call it quits, and beam Himself right on out of this crazy world, but He didn't. He loved us so He waited. He wasn't dragging His feet and whining along the way; no, He prayed, worshiped, lived fully present in the moment. He went about His life living out the purposes of the Father in the everyday. He was faithful all the way to the cross, a long and awaited moment.

I want to work out my waiting muscles, don't you? What fun it would be to have Mary, Hannah, Rebekah, and Sarah and the rest of the biblical girl gang over for coffee and just hear their stories. To glean from their testament of integrity and strength in their waiting and to come and cheer us on in ours. These women were no more special, gifted, or loved than me and you. This faithful, trusting, and joyful waiting they lived out is totally within our capacity as well if we choose it. Remember the characteristics of holy grit? Let's add waiting well to that list.

We took California off the shelf multiple times over the five years we served in Amsterdam. Every year we would pull it down, pray, wait, and God would say not yet, trust me. Until one day His answer changed.

Three months before I gave birth to Emma, I felt for the first time that God was shifting something about California. Up until then, it was just a deep knowing in my spirit that we would one day be there. But on that day something felt different, like a door was suddenly open and there was a sense of release. All day I couldn't shake the feeling, but I wanted to wait for the right moment to talk to Josh about it. (A girl's got to plan out these kinds of things.) That night Josh and I were giving the girls a bath when we both oddly looked at each other. It was that, "Are you feeling what I'm feeling?" type of look. God had been speaking to both of us that day, if you can believe it. We knew it was finally time. The waiting was over, the dream was not abandoned—California came off the shelf.

Walk in His Blessing

We have an incredible advantage as Christ followers when it comes to seasons of waiting. God knows what is to come, and He sets a course with our best in mind. The timing of our move allowed us to be with my family during the pandemic. It gave us the opportunity to build our own business that would support our life in California. God prepared our hearts and character for thriving in a new place with deeper assignments. When we yield to His timing, we walk in His blessing.

If we had forced the California dream before it was time, we would have missed out on all the blessings God had for us in Amsterdam and in Oklahoma. Looking back at those times I am so thankful God made His timing and pace for the California dream clear to us so we could walk with Him. God often reveals one step at a time for us rather than the whole picture, which can sometimes be frustrating, but it is a great way of learning how to be completely dependent on Him and His timing.

If you are waiting on the dream, the yes for a move, or the release of a promise, hold fast to the God who has good plans for you, who is after the best outcome for your life. Trust His timing, and your path will flourish.

CHAPTER THIRTEEN

Real Rest

In the summer of 2021, our best friends invited us to join them for a couples' vacation in Florida: "Guys, it's a four-million-dollar home on the beach, white sand, clear water… no kids." We said yes on the spot. With babysitters on hand and bags packed, we spent a week in a stunning home on the beach front. They weren't lying. The sand was white, and the air was fresh. The mornings were slow and sweet like honey; we drank our coffee before it went cold and sipped wine as the sun set. Of course, we tried all the brunch spots and more than our share of banana pudding ice cream. We slept deep and long. It was bliss.

I went on the trip looking for a reset. I had been so tired with the demands of everyday life and needed a break. In that grand house in Florida, I found serenity, peace, and—not to be dramatic or anything—I'm pretty sure I was glowing. I was confident that the "mom Lexi" that had left Tulsa one week prior was not the same one coming back. Lo and behold I found my sharp mind, good posture, and dare I say my patience on the beach. I was eager to bring all that goodness back home to my kids. My friend, Ajiah, and I agreed that with this recharge, we would finally be the slow to anger, gentle, and loving mothers we had always wanted to be. We had no stress, we had adapted to the island ways, and we were changed women, thank you very much.

Hand to heart, on our first morning back home I woke up with everything *but* the fruits of gentleness, being slow to anger, and patience. Not to mention, my mom brain and bad posture had already returned. My phone began to buzz; it was Ajiah. I answered and could hear the echoes of her kids crying in the background. We didn't say a word. We didn't have to. Finally, I broke the silence, "I thought we were rested! I thought a vacation was going to give us days if not weeks of peace before tapering off!" Life came and knocked us right back to reality. And there I was again, tired to the bone.

More people in America are reporting feeling chronically tired, burned out, and fatigued. Largely speaking, the mental health of the American people is at an all-time low.[3] We are tired, and our souls are aching for real rest. This restlessness we feel goes far beyond mental and physical fatigue but rather is found deep in our core. A restlessness that is burrowed in, manifesting into stress, health issues, emotional paralysis, confusion, and long-term burnout. It's a serious epidemic in our society today and will become an issue we pass down to the next generation unless we learn to overcome it now.

And the truth is that the chronic restlessness we are feeling isn't being fixed with organic green juice and meditation. More caffeine isn't helping, more money isn't doing it, more career success isn't lightening the load. A nap isn't cutting it. A sabbatical isn't curing the burnout within the Church. A weekend off isn't enough. *A mansion on the white beaches of Seaside isn't cutting it.* Rest is physical and spiritual work, and it is what will propel us forward on our journey with God.

Our Restless Hearts

Our desire for soulful rest can only be remedied by one source, the true giver of spiritual rest, Jesus. Jesus was aware of every struggle we would face in our lifetime and spoke straight to our

---

3   American Psychiatric Association, "Annual mental health poll reveals increasing anxiety among U.S. adults," 2024.

problem with a word that goes beyond time. I want you to read the verses below found in Matthew 11:28-30 and insert your name in the blank. I'm referencing the Message translation for a more conversational tone. These words from Jesus are for you *today.*

> _____, *are you tired? Worn out? Burned out on religion? Come to me,* _____. *Get away with me and you'll recover your life.* _____, *I'll show you how to take a real rest. Walk with me and work with me—watch how I do it. Learn the unforced rhythms of grace. I won't lay anything heavy or ill-fitting on you.* _____, *keep company with me and you'll learn to live freely and lightly.*

His words here are my favorite. His invitation to *real* rest is salve to my tired soul. Isn't this truly the desire we are all craving? To find rest that sustains us way past the sleepless nights and long hours of the day? I love that Jesus is inviting us to walk with Him and learn the unforced rhythms of grace. He promises that while we walk closely with Him, we will be blessed. As we pursue the act of abiding in His presence and cultivating a deeper connection to His Spirit, we will begin to awaken out of the sleepiness in our souls. He tells us His path is full of grace and will lead us to a place of peace and spiritual rest. And I love this: "keep company with me, and you will learn to live lightly and freely." Yes and amen. Lightly and freely are music to my ears. This way of life isn't void of problems, but it gives us the ability to be surrounded by His love and grace in the process, and that takes us out of heaviness and captivity and into a life lived lightly and freely. There is one source of rest and it is walking in the company of Jesus, day by day, in step with His grace.

Y'all, my spirit has been to the point of complete exhaustion… has yours? I have gone through many seasons in my life where I was drawing water from all kinds of wells that were shallow and full of gunk. We are consuming water from a source full of striving, comparison, fear of man, and all the other junk that is toxic to our spirits. If we keep on going to the same well, pulling up water from the same sources that only make us more weak, more tired, and emptier, we will keep being thirsty and never quenched.

In John 4 we read the precious story of the woman at the well. We do not know her name, but I can't fathom the moment she had at that well with Jesus. After she questioned why He would ask her for water with she being a Samaritan and He being a Jew (a social no-no in that day), He answered,

Everyone who drinks this water will be thirsty again, but whoever drinks the water I give them will never thirst. Indeed, the water I give them will become in them a spring of water welling up to eternal life.

This is her moment. The moment that Jesus is inviting her to a life of fellowship and discipleship with Him. Offering the true source of fulfillment for her soul. This ordinary woman, who is nameless in the scriptures, believed Jesus was the Messiah and went on to share about Him to her people. It says that many came to believe in Jesus because of the word of her testimony. She heard and saw that the Living Water, the true source of salvation, rest, peace and joy, was alive, and she said yes to following Him.

Jesus is the Living Water and all who are thirsty can come and be thirsty no more. All who are desperate for rest can find true rest in His presence. This is the only source that will truly fill our weary minds and hearts. We are trying to fix our spiritual angst, restlessness, and fatigue with man-made sources that have a high investment cost and no return. True rest comes from Jesus, our source of living water.

We've talked a lot about the importance and power of abiding in Christ. And on this topic of rest it is clear that it applies. When we are "in company" with Jesus we are on the path to learning the unforced rhythms of rest. What does He mean by unforced? He means that we walk with ease, full of His grace. It means that even in the hard work and strenuous times we carry a supernatural ease of walking closely with Jesus.

The Importance of Sabbath

How do we enter in to more spiritual rest? Through times of daily prayer, Scripture study, and worship, and making time to declare that God is the source of provision for you and that He is faithful over your time and life. In the Bible we learn of Sabbath, a weekly practice of rest that serves as a rhythm for rest in our week.

As we walk daily in company with Jesus we also have the opportunity to practice Sabbath. Mark 2:27 says, "The Sabbath was made for man, and not man for the Sabbath." God ordained Sabbath as holy and good *after* He created man. We are not slaves to Sabbath, but it is a gift to us. God knew that our hard work requires first and foremost spiritual rest in abiding in Jesus but also physical rest.

Sabbath is one of the most anti-cultural acts of obedience we find in the Bible. Sabbath is a spiritual declaration that says, "I trust God's will to be done, and I can rest in that assurance." In a world that is constantly encouraging us to run faster, harder, and longer, Sabbath waves the white flag and calls us to surrender.

The world says to outrun the girl next to you, but God's kingdom and His way say you don't have to rush and strive to get ahead. You don't have to worry and stress about not running your race fast enough, hard enough, or early enough. The line to the calling on your life and the dream in your heart is zero, people. No one else gets to line up for your calling. That is a spot reserved for you and you alone, anointed and appointed by God. Friend, you can *rest*. You can move at the pace and in the way God has asked you to without the possibility or fear that someone will get there first.

We need to choose to see Sabbath as more than just a discipline to mark off the list, but rather as a spiritual declaration that says, "I am walking in the company of God, and I don't need to push harder to claim my place. I can actually rest assured that God's way is far better than my way. Honoring God by honoring Sabbath will only propel me further into my purpose, not away from it. God's kingdom is upside down in this world, and His ways are off beat to the world's ways."

Sabbath is more than just an hour on a Sunday morning. Sabbath is so much more than just a ritual that does not carry any real weight or purpose to our week. Sabbath is a God-ordained time set apart for our spiritual, mental, and physical rest to align our heart to God's unforced rhythms of grace in our lives. Sabbath is more than Sunday clothes with donuts in the foyer. Sabbath is the soul declaration of a life that is surrendered and fully trusting in God's path, pace, and purpose. We are not in a rush because God holds every moment of our lives, and we are not striving because God already holds all power and authority over every step He planned out for us before we were even born. We can walk in grace, breathing deeply, resting in His faithfulness, and full of assurance in our path. That is the power of choosing to walk with Jesus.

Our Bodies Are Temples

Do you see how the cure to our chronic restlessness, the gnawing ache in our soul, is Jesus? Only His rest can penetrate the deep restlessness we suffer from. His peace replaces our worry, His grace surpasses our striving, and His faithfulness is far more powerful than any amount of extra hours we can clock in. While Jesus heals the tiredness we feel in our souls, He also has something to say about how we take care of our physical bodies. We have been called to a long obedience, a life of walking with God and serving Him in the mighty ways He is laying before you. The worst thing we can do is miss out on the fullness of that calling because we can't physically do the work.

Taking care of our bodies and health is a less talked about importance in our walk with God. We must be equipped to run the race Jesus is setting before us. Our body is the vehicle that carries us through every magnificent season this life holds. Our body is our house, how we feel, how we move, how we experience this whole world around us. Our bodies, even when they are broken, operate by the grace of God with every breath.

And now that I am in my thirties I've learned that what used to work no longer works. Gone are the days I could stay up late and not pay for it. Gone are the days I could eat an orange and kick a cold. Now, I wake up and my body cracks in seven places. If I don't eat three meals a day and rely on the power of a caffeinated beverage, I will in fact pass out. Taking care of my body is important because I have three little girls who need me well, a husband I love, and a calling I would like to be physically and spiritually energized for. We have so many physical limitations, and as we get older we come across more physical challenges.

I am not by any means a workout instructor, diet adviser, or health mentor, but it's common sense that if our bodies are our vehicle to run the race before us, we have a responsibility to take care of them. We won't always get this right, but are we making better decisions for ourselves with what is in our control? Are we treating our bodies as sacred, holy, and valuable to our life and calling?

While vacations, sabbaticals, weekend getaways, and retreats are wonderful and needed, they are not the answer to rest and peace. Achieving long rest and peace so we can do the work we have been called to do requires us to learn to rest *in* our daily life, not when we are out of it.

A few ways we can do this. This is an ongoing list, so see this as a starting place to get the wheels turning. My advice is to implement one and add and adjust as you go. The goal is to add rhythms of reflection and rest as you commit to the daily rest of walking with the source of rest, Jesus.

For weekly rest, I urge you to decide as a family when you can take a step back from your daily work and commit a day of Sabbath to God. Many of my ministry friends take a Sabbath on Friday because Sunday mornings are part of their work hours. Set aside the demands, and align your spirit to worship and praise God, putting trust in His plan, pace, and path. Consider using this day to take a social media break or making it a "no tech" day. Think about ways to eliminate distractions from the day and focus more on meeting with Jesus. Our Sabbath in this period of life looks like worshiping with our church family in the morning, putting away electronics and spending the day as a family at the park, and having a special dinner in the evening. It's, of course, loud, messy, and chaotic, but it's a discipline we want to honor in our home the best we can. Josh and I use bits of the day or after the kids are asleep to chat briefly about how God has been faithful to us and what we are thankful for presently.

Along with Sabbath, plan a quarterly or yearly getaway for you or you and your spouse to reflect and pray on what God has done. Use this time to take inventory of your home, work, and how you're walking out your values as a family together and personally. Taking time to reflect on a season and plan for the next is a great way to keep on track with the path God has for you. This is a time to relax and enjoy, and a time to look forward to in busy seasons. But don't make the same mistake I did with expecting a getaway to be a substitute for spiritual rest. These mini retreats to reflect and plan for the future are practical ways to set yourself up for success in your home and calling as a family and personally. Good intentions will get you nowhere without a plan and clear direction.

And here are a few ways we can unclog our brain during the week and add more peace and rest to our body, mind, and soul. Turn off your phone an hour before bed. Set a tech limit. Be with people, get outside, and get good sleep. Don't wing it—make a plan and set it in motion. The thing to remember is that we can do all these things but not receive true rest if we leave out the source of true rest. Keep the first thing first, and then add in ways to support your mental, physical, and emotional health.

Learning to be a woman who rests well has been a battle for me. When I was forced to rest due to sickness, burnout, or postpartum, I always experienced heavy levels of stress. To stop, slow down, and be still was hard for me. Putting on the brakes felt like failure and a sign of weakness. Resting made me feel worse and antsy. It was a vicious cycle and I was the hamster trapped on the spinning wheel.

Truth was, I felt most valuable when I was producing, achieving, and checking off my list. If I could be of service, growing, or making my way forward, then I would be happy. At least happier. Eventually I would work myself emotionally and physically to the point of burnout and develop some strange stress tick or headache that would force me to slow down.

So I would take the absolute minimum required time to rest, and the moment I was a tiny bit better, I was back at it with the same unhealthy rhythms of constant business and work and progress and an, "I'll rest when I'm dead" gung-ho attitude. So much of my identity was rooted in what I did, not who I was. I was constantly moving and achieving to find validation and love from others and myself.

I needed God's truth over my identity in those times. I believed my value was in what I produced, but God said I was already valued because I was His image bearer. I didn't have to work for love or acceptance—I was already fully loved. When this really sunk into my heart I began to view rest in a new way. Choosing to walk in the opposite spirit, rest became my act of worship and assurance of who I was in Christ. It became spiritual warfare over my identity and place in Christ.

It became so apparent to me that rest was my friend not my enemy that I incorporated moments of spiritual and physical rest into my day. At 7:00 p.m. I declared the day over. I would stop housework, put the kids to bed, and call it a day. If the dishes were in the sink, that was OK. I was a good mom even if the house was a little messy. If I didn't finish everything I wanted to, that was OK, too. It was time to shower, read a bit (a personal joy of mine), and get some sleep. My work was not the measuring stick of my worth.

Rest is physical and spiritual work. It takes practice to build the discipline of rest into our lives. As we choose physical moments of rest we must also lean into our spiritual rest of choosing trust in God. Our mission will only grow and prosper as we develop a stronger and more active discipline of rest in our lives. It is the rest that will propel us forward with restoration and perseverance, and rest will be our anthem of praise and trust in a world that is working so dang hard to achieve.

God's timing for the dreams He places in our hearts doesn't usually follow the timeline we think it should. Walking with God means following His pace, letting Him set the tempo, and trying not to run ahead. When we take His dream for us and try to accomplish it on our own, we end up going down paths that weren't meant for us. Only through denying our own timelines and embracing God's can we experience the fullness of the plan He has for us. It may not make complete sense to us in the moment, but in time, we will begin to see how wise and good God is for the pace He sets for our path.

PART 4: PROVISION

TRUSTING GOD
FULLY TO HELP
US FULFILL
OUR PURPOSE

Grace Alone

I started writing this book when Emma was three months old. She just turned five a few weeks ago. It didn't take me this long because I didn't have the time or the help to make the time; it took this long because of a series of very unfortunate events that turned into one long telenovela of my life. I was a victim to postpartum depression and anxiety. I knew what postpartum was, but I didn't know what postpartum was. It would be months until I realized what was happening and eventually got the help I needed. The depression and anxiety spiraled during COVID-19, and what started small turned chronic.

Doing daily tasks felt over my head, and doing the things I loved, like writing, felt like swimming against the current. I found myself sinking deep into the couch while my kids played or watched TV. I was watching my life, almost like a movie, unable to actually feel anything. I felt guilty for being this way. I was back in my hometown with my family, we had purchased a home for a steal, Josh had a great job, and we were expecting God to move us to California. My kids were healthy and thriving. And I was so incredibly sad.

When my postpartum depression was at its worst COVID-19 hit. What was hard became impossible. For those who know me and saw me during this period of time, you would probably say you couldn't tell I was depressed. Sad sometimes, maybe. But the thing about emotional and mental pain is that it can be masked and hidden. Most of my hiding was due to not wanting to accept it. I was in denial that I felt this terrible and felt deeply guilty for feeling the way I did.

It wouldn't be until three years later that I felt like myself again. Even today I have to fight for my peace, protect it, and actively pursue rest to not fall back into that place. Now I have systems, rhythms, and people to help me thrive and not hide. But it took a long time to get here.

In the middle of this mental and emotional battle, I still knew I was called to write this book. At first I put it on hold so I could get back to a new normal with all that life was throwing at me. I needed to focus on my health and, for the love, figure out this COVID-19 thing. In the middle of it all, God was walking me through a journey of listening and obeying His call, and as a family we were taking the steps to obey God by moving to California. My life was in surrender to obedience. And now, my emotional and mental health was in that process of surrendering obedience to Him as well.

What I found out was that depression and anxiety doesn't just magically go away overnight. Day by day, month by month, it was getting more manageable as I learned the tools to handle it. Even today I wrestle with the daily pull to fall back into anxiety. It is a daily, sometimes minute-by-minute awareness that I face. I am not immune to downright bad days of feeling over-stimulated, anxious, and sad. Even on good days these feelings can come barging in, demanding to take over.

The difference between then and now? My eyes are wide open to the power and gift of grace. Not Grace as in the girl we all knew growing up who loved horses and had long, brown, wavy hair and a knack for Bible memorization. We all know that girl, and gosh, don't we love her? But grace, the supernatural gift God Himself offers us when we meet our end and His ability begins. Grace takes us from what we alone are capable of to what we are capable of only through the grace of God. We need God's moment-to-moment presence in our lives. It is only through His grace that we are able to fulfill His calling for us.

Daily Presence of God

In the Lord's Prayer (Matthew 6:9-13) God acknowledges our need for His daily grace. When we pray, give us our daily bread—this points to our daily provision, such as food and clothing, as well as our daily need for God's presence, grace, and mercy. We are all facing challenges and adversaries in our daily lives and journey of faith. Our Heavenly Father has asked us to pray for the daily provision needed to be faithful to Him where we are. He does not instruct us to pray for His annually, monthly, or weekly provision, but daily, moment-by-moment provision. How beautiful is that? God knows that to walk in obedience and fully experience the plans He has for us requires a daily relationship and a daily petition for His provision in our lives.

Second Corinthians 9:8 says, "And God is able to bless you abundantly, so that in all things at all times, having all that you need, you will abound in every good work."

God's daily bread is to sustain you to do the work He has set before you. His daily provision for us is sufficient for the long haul. Just like we need food and water to sustain our bodies, we need the daily presence and grace of God to sustain us for our daily spiritual nourishment. If we are choosing God's path for our lives, we must also choose God's source of provision. His way requires His daily bread to supply the physical needs and spiritual food we need to endure and run the race set before us.

We are currently in a series at our home church in California about the early Church we see in the book of Acts. What started as a small group of men and women following Jesus, learning to live like Him and love like Him, turned into a movement. After

His resurrection the early Church was born. I love that God chose Mary, the woman Jesus saved from demonic oppression when they first met, to be the one to proclaim the good news of Jesus' resurrection first. If Jesus' resurrection was a farce, surely no one would have come up with a woman being the first to declare He was risen. But God, He chose a woman.

From that moment on the early Church gathered and began to figure out how to do this thing called life on mission with each other. They appointed leaders and caretakers; everyone had a role to play and it was all done within the context of community. The Church was flesh and blood, not real estate.

The trials the early Church faced were brutal at times. The early Christians would go by two into towns and preach the good news of Jesus, often being thrown out, imprisoned, or killed. The opposition was savage and unpredictable, but Jesus had told the early church they would face trials and that He had already overcome them. It was by grace alone that they tapped into supernatural peace and boldness of faith.

We first and foremost have the gift of grace through salvation. Through the death and resurrection of Jesus we, by faith and through grace, are forgiven of our sins and will be in unhindered communion with God for eternity. The grace of salvation is the greatest gift of all for us as believers. By God's grace we have been saved. By God's grace we have been redeemed. By God's grace we are co-heirs with Christ, no longer separated by sin but restored fully and eternally to our Father in heaven. Amen! What grace has done is saved, delivered, and freed us from all bondage of sin and death. Without the grace of God, without the gift of salvation we would be yet still orphans, separated and wandering.

God in His grace offers salvation to us all. The good news of the gospel is not off limits to anyone. All are welcome to receive the grace of God; grace is for all of us. God's grace also secures our salvation. We no longer live under the law of Moses but by the atonement of grace through faith. God knew our sin would always result in us falling short of His glory; even the law could not overcome it. But grace sure does, and what a gift it is.

Secondly, grace comes in the form of the Holy Spirit, who enables us to do the work set before us.

But he said to me, "My grace is sufficient for you, for my power is made perfect in weakness." Therefore I will boast all the more gladly about my weaknesses, so that Christ's power may rest on me. That is why, for Christ's sake, I delight in weaknesses, in insults, in hardships, in persecutions, in difficulties. For when I am weak, then I am strong (2 Corinthians 12:9–10).

The fuel to grace is—drumroll, please—our weaknesses! God is strong and mighty when we have reached our end. I grew up playing Mario Kart and you could unlock the ability to get a "booster." You would be going at full speed, but once you unlocked that booster you went flying beyond your own ability. This is grace—it is supercharged in our weakness. Not only does grace save us, but it enables us to go and do the work and run the race set before us! It is through the grace of God and His Holy Spirit that we can overcome all things and see victory in all things God hands to us.

This is especially relevant and apparent as we pursue our God-dreams. If we believe for one second that this dream will be a hit and a success due to our own power and talent, we are wrong. God-dreams require God-sized grace. It is when we find ourselves standing in the face of a dream that is too big, over our pay grade, and out of our league that God's grace swoops in and enables us.

Today as I sit here in the parking lot of my kids' gymnastics class, I can tell you it is by grace alone that this book is in your hands. Right now it's on a Google Doc on my phone, but by grace you hold it presently. There is no way my own tired, thirty-something mom bod that gets dizzy without a snack every twenty minutes and is prone to allergies has the mental strength through mom brain to write all these words. Let alone wake up early, put three meals on the table, and parent all day long. There is no world where I am going to be able to do that if it wasn't for the living and abundant grace of God in my life.

And you, my friend, I'm sure are facing battles seen and unseen every day. There are wars you are fighting physically, spiritually, emotionally, and mentally. We all need God's good grace to help us moment by moment. The calling God has set before you is in fact attainable and achievable with and by God's grace. God's grace will be in step with you as you do your everyday life stuff and as you move the needle inch by inch in your God-given dreams.

I told my husband recently I finally understood why God has called me to the things He has called me to now instead of earlier in my life. Wouldn't it have been so much easier for me to do these things ten years ago? But I realize that just as important is who we become in the process. It is through the work, the resistance, the opposition that we must learn to step into grace and keep our eyes up. If it were a different time and place our character wouldn't experience the growth God has in store for us.

The process of our obedience and surrender is equally as important for the sake of character building, becoming holy in Christ, and knowing deeper who God is. God is after both: the outer work and the inner.

Grace is Not Passive

We can and should expect resistance to come as we pursue obedience toward the things God has for us. This is a given. Opposition is coming your way the moment you say yes to God. This is a pill we need to learn how to swallow now instead of trying to live this life of following Jesus and also staying on good terms with everyone. We cannot follow God's path and also keep everyone happy. We cannot follow God's path and also not step on anyone's toes. The world opposes Jesus, therefore, as Christ followers, we, too, will be opposed.

Opposition in our calling can come in all shapes and sizes. It might mean you are the only one who has convictions that aren't in alignment with those around you. It may look like moving when it doesn't make sense to others. It might be battling health and mental struggles. Not all opposition is a direct demonic assault, but we live in a world that promises challenges in our health, our bodies, our minds, and our relationships. No one is exempt from opposition, especially those going against the spiritual forces that oppose Jesus.

Paul understood this power of grace and spoke of boasting in the grace and power of God. He knew it was by God's saving grace and enabling grace that he was who he was and was able to do what he was called to do.

So what does this mean for you today? It means everything. Whatever you are facing—the mountain ahead of you, the dream that feels far away, the lack of understanding, the opposition you face—God's grace is sufficient even still. If you are feeling unable, tired, and weak, that's OK. Grace is made powerful in our weaknesses. This is the very soil in which grace grows and flourishes in our lives.

But how do we obtain grace? Yes, grace has been freely given, but there's more to it than that. Paul even says, "But by the grace of God I am what I am, and his grace toward me was not in vain. On the contrary, I worked harder than any of them, though it was not I, but the grace of God that is with me" (1 Corinthians 15:10, ESV).

But what is grace sparked by? What empowers grace to move actively in our lives and circumstances?

For the grace of God has appeared that offers salvation to all people. It teaches us to say "No" to ungodliness and worldly passions, and to live self-controlled, upright and godly lives in this present age, while we wait for the blessed hope—the appearing of the glory of our great God and Savior, Jesus Christ, who gave himself for us to redeem us from all wickedness and to purify for himself a people that are his very own, eager to do what is good (Titus 2:11–14).

Through saving grace, which we received through Jesus, we are activated to pursue holiness and godliness. Like it says in the scripture, "training us to renounce ungodliness and worldly passions, and to live self-controlled, upright, and godly lives in the present age." Let's add that grace saves us and instructs us how to live. As Christians who have received the grace of salvation, it is shown through our decision to love as Christ instructs, surrendered to His will and way.

Here's what I learned to be true while I faced opposition in my calling: eyes up. When my eyes are focused on Christ and I am actively pursuing a relationship with Him, seeking to walk in holiness and obedience to His way of life, the grace to go into wherever He has called me to is possible.

Here is what I am not saying. I am not saying that if you just prayed harder, you wouldn't be depressed. If you just had more faith, you would see the miracle. If you could just behave more like a Christian, then you would see a breakthrough. What

I am saying is that grace has been given, and, in the same breath, grace is not passive.

As we seek holiness and relationship with the Father, grace is a side effect. Just like abiding in God's Word gives us peace, hope, and direction, grace is the overflow of actively obeying and walking in God's Word.

Imagine you are standing in front of a glorious mountain. The lush greenery covers it like a blanket, the top disappearing into the clouds. There is a trail that is meant for you winding all the way up. That trail is your path of obedience toward the goodness God has for you. But you realize you have never trained for a long hike like this before. Not only that, you get winded after a brisk walk around Target. How on earth will you scale this mountain? Surely you will slip and fall. Surely you will get dehydrated and give up. But God beckons you to climb the mountain.

Then Jesus shows up and says, "Don't worry, I am the Way to the Father, and I also know the way up this mountain. Trust Me." You trust Him, but you still can't get your head around how you will overcome all the challenges that are ahead in this climb.

Grace comes in at this moment as a gift. It holds the space for you to overcome challenges, experience supernatural peace, and have a supernatural ability to do the impossible. But grace isn't unlocked as you stand at the foothill; it's active and real, but it only works when you begin the hike. So you start, one foot in front of the other, eyes on Jesus, walking as He walks, placing your feet where He places His. You move like Him and obtain His habits, rhythms, and ways. And as you do, grace takes your human ability and brings you the power, ability, resources, and peace through the Holy Spirit.

As you follow, as you begin, grace is activated. When God says move, grace enables us to move. When God says stop and rest, grace is there, too.

The Power in Grace

When we speak of grace we might as well be speaking of power. Grace often gets a gentle and, well, graceful rep. But grace is power, the power to do all things through God's strength despite our own. Grace is God's natural power activated within us to do good works.

Over the past few years as I've wrestled through the hormone mania that is postpartum and recovery, I have received help from hormone doctors, therapists, and the spiritual community. But let me say this: while yes, we absolutely need the help of doctors and therapists and a strong community on this journey, there is no amount of therapy or supplements that will make up for the grace needed to do the thing you have been called to do.

God called you, and only His grace can sustain you and equip you. His calling will require faith and grace from the source of the dream, in Christ alone. It will be messy and far from a straight line beginning to end, but it will come with character, perseverance, hope, and a deeper knowing of Jesus. And we know now that abundant life is found in the middle of those things.

There is nothing we have been called to do that can be done in our own strength. All work assigned from God requires the grace and power to accomplish it. This is good news for us, friends. It isn't up to us! We can rest in knowing God will supply us with what is needed to complete the good works set before us. It is not dependent on us but on our obedience and God's grace.

I can't imagine the circumstances that are opposing you in this season of life. I'm sure if we were able to be face to face we could let each other into our worlds for a moment and share the challenges and the things that feel too heavy and wide that stand between us and our calling. You know what that thing is.

For me it's been postpartum, and it's been feeling underqualified when I compare myself to other women around me. I've experienced opposition in the form of book proposal rejections, lots of them. Opposition when it comes to finances, time, health problems, and family dynamics. Opposition will come, but God has already prepared the grace necessary for you when it does. All you have to do is say yes, walk in obedience, and keep your eyes up. Step by step, grace by grace, until our whole life sings of His glory to the very end.

Made for Relationship

Like I said before, I was homeschooled from second grade all the way to my high school graduation. It was there in the co-op groups and field trips that I was first shown what a village looked like. My mom and her friends, only in their early thirties at the time, braved the unknown territory of "homeschooling." These women said, "Let's do this. And let's do it together."

And that they did. My educational background holds the faces of many women other than just my mom. They would pick out curriculums together, and when they couldn't find one they liked they would write one themselves. They planned out whose house all the kids would go to and who would teach what subject. We carpooled, shared pantries, passed around clothes, and slept over at each other's houses. These women held my hair back when I was sick, put Band-Aids on my knees, and never ran out of hugs and advice. They taught me, led me, fed me, formed me, and raised me. All of them, together.

It's always the women.

I said yes because they did first. Their strength, courage, and willingness to do hard and holy things planted the same strengths within me from a young age. We are a combination of the people we surround ourselves with, and I'm the mom and friend and wife I am today—the good parts, at least—largely because of them.

It's wild to think about my mom and her friends today and realize they were in their late twenties and early thirties when they began their friendships. They banded together because they knew that life and raising kids and being married and maintaining who they were was impossible without confidantes. They needed each other, and it was within the village they made that they thrived. I watched them cry and laugh and vent to one another over sodas while I played on jungle gyms. I heard my mom comforting her friends over the phone late at night, spinning the cord in her fingers. I watched as they pulled out pouches of juice and Lunchables from coolers on field trips.

They showed me early on that life wasn't meant to be done alone. In order to thrive we need the support and solidarity that comes with deep and meaningful friendships, the ride or dies, the call-you-uppers, the I've-got-yous, the your-mess-is-my-mess friends.

It is woven within our DNA by the Creator to need and thrive within relationships. Life in any capacity was never intended to be done alone. We see in Genesis that God saw Adam and said it was not good for him to be alone. God, being three in One, models the perfect vision of community. It is no wonder that within us, His image bearers, we are made to live life within the context of relationship as well.

Three Types of Spiritual Relationships

I can hear my father-in-law's voice saying, "Life is about relationships." He likes to remind us all as often as possible of this truth. God cares deeply about our friendships, and He understands the depth of importance they have when it comes to the overall health of our lives and in our journey of saying yes to our God-dream. Healthy relationships provide different values depending on the type of relationship. One way to view the types of relationships that bring value to our lives is through the over, side to side, and reaching back.

"Looking up" relationships are toward those people who are wiser and further along than us. These are the people whose character we really appreciate and want to model. These are our gems. Our mentors, parents, pastors, coaches, teachers, or friends who are a few seasons ahead of us in life and have already gone through the hard work. These are the people we are looking up to and learning from.

Then we have our side-to-siders. In this group you're going to find the people you do a lot of day-to-day life with. These are the folks who are in the trenches with you. The ones you are in the same boat with, navigating life experiences in similar waves. These friendships offer companionship, understanding, and walking through discipleship at roughly the same pace. We live life side by side, learning, growing, and experiencing life together.

Lastly, the reach behind-ers. Josh and I spent the first five years of our marriage doing a lot of this work. We led and staffed ministry schools that required lots of time sitting down with people younger than us or in seasons of life behind us, discipling them toward Jesus. I was their "lookupper'" relationship, and they were my "reach behind" relationships. To disciple someone, meaning to urge them on in their relationship with Jesus and point them continuously back to Him and His Word, is some of the most rewarding and best work. In these relationships we are fulfilling our call to disciple, as well as taking the opportunity to recall God in our own story. When we get to look back and wave a hand to those further behind us, we are waving the flag of God's promises, shouting His goodness, and offering our testaments of His faithfulness.

These three types of relationships are crucial to our spiritual journey and fulfillment in life. Each offers us a unique and beautiful part to play in our walk with God. The homeschool moms I mentioned were the ones I looked at ahead of me. They were raising the flag and shouting God's character, pointing me to Jesus even when I was distracted and too much of a kid to really care. My side-to-side friend circle used to be big and wide as a teenager and has turned into a very small group of women. With the added responsibilities over the years, instead of spreading thin I have nurtured a few deep, long friendships. These girls know how I'm doing based on the tone of my voice, and they have heard my deepest secrets, my fears, and my pain points. They encourage me when Josh and I aren't having a good day, fight for me when I'm down, pray for me, push me, challenge me, laugh and cry and watch reality television with me. Side-by-siders, the bread-and-butter friendships. And while I no longer work in full-time ministry, I'm reaching back and pouring into my three little girls, my greatest mission field. When I can, I keep my door open for girls at church to come over for a chat or host a small group Bible study.

It is evident in the Bible that surrendering to God and choosing God's way means choosing to live life in community. We see in the Bible that Jesus talks about how we as Christ followers are one body: "For just as each of us has one body with many members, and these members do not all have the same function, so in Christ we, though many, form one body, and each member belongs to all the others" (Romans 12:4–5). We all serve in different ways, each just as important. If one of us hurts, we all hurt. If one part of the body is unhealthy, we all feel it. If one part of the body believes another part is cooler or more important and also wants to be an ear or whatever, well, then we are insufficient in another area. We all need each other, not only for our personal gain but for the body as a whole. When we each walk in obedience and we each play our part, the church thrives.

God loves relationships. He has built us to thrive in relationship with Him and with each other. Proverbs 27:9 says, "The heartfelt counsel of a friend is as sweet as perfume and incense" (NLT). Relationships make life sweet and rough times bearable. Friendships, whether we are looking up, looking to our side, or reaching behind, help us thrive in this one glorious life.

Even Introverts Need Community

If you're an introvert like me this is your least favorite chapter. I am a homebody to my core. When plans are canceled, I rejoice. When I have nothing scheduled for the week, I will gladly stay in my sweats and stay indoors. People never believe me when I tell them I am an introvert, because I get along with people really easily. I love being with people, but gosh, it drains me. To recharge, I need to lock myself in my room for an entire night and not speak or hang with anyone except myself. My husband, on the other hand, goes crazy if he's alone for five minutes. The guy needs parties, events, noise, food, and friends every day.

But even girls like me, who need to retreat more than others, who get social anxiety like I do, and who fill their tank by being away from others, deeply need connection. It takes more work for me to pursue God's way in this area. When I say yes to hosting, to going to the party, to showing up dressed and ready to connect on Sunday mornings or whatever it may be, I always leave encouraged. The times I want to be alone and instead pursue community, I am filled in a way that reminds me that I in fact need people even if it takes energy to show up. It's worth showing up when it feels like staying home.

I'm not saying you never recharge or retreat. You absolutely take that time and set healthy boundaries, but to say no to healthy friendships, mentors, and face-to-face community is detrimental to our spiritual growth. Why? Because we are made by and for relationships. You don't have to turn into someone you're not to say yes to relationships. You can be fully yourself, honest and transparent where you're at, *and* make time to nurture friendships and bring people into your process and journey with God. Being a homebody, introvert, not so crazy about going out past 7:00 p.m. kind of girl isn't a flaw. It just means that God's grace is needed in this area for you a bit more than others. And on the other end of the spectrum, you may be the type who recharges and thrives doing all the things with people every day. While this is amazing, God may need to help you build deeper and more intentional friendships. Either way, the act of pursuing relationships in this life is a good cause.

A beautiful example of friendship in the Bible is found in Ruth 1:16. Ruth and her mother-in-law, Naomi, find themselves widows. Naomi chooses not to return to her hometown but instead to pursue a place where God is worshiped, knowing she will be a foreigner, never to marry again. Noami urges Ruth to go back home so she can start a new life, and Ruth's response is this, "But Ruth replied, 'Don't urge me to leave you or to turn back from you. Where you go I will go, and where you stay I will stay. Your people will be my people and your God my God.'"

Funny enough, Josh and I recited those words to each other in our marriage vows, and while that is all good and beautiful and true, Ruth didn't share those words of fierce companionship with a spouse, she shared them with her mother-in-law, her close friend. What a gift to have a friend like Ruth and to be a friend like her.

Come As You Are

This work of finding friends, building a community of other men and women around you spurring you on in your race toward God's highest purpose for your life is not always easy. Some of the very worst pain can come from the sting of a failed community. For many of us it was our closest friends who betrayed us. Finding friends can feel a lot like online dating, awkward and like the Wild Wild West. And as we get older it can become more complicated with time and proximity and yada yada yada.

Loneliness can be a dark and painful road. It highlights the need for belonging and companionship in life. While social media and other forms of connecting online are meant to bring us together at the click of a button, these forms of connection are, at their core, synthetic. Nothing can take the place of the real thing. In a world that has promised more connection, more exposure, and has offered an abundance of easy interaction to each other, we are still lonely, depressed, and anxious.[4]

True connection is in sitting down together, eye contact, physical touch, and sharing time and space. To be a woman who fights for meals around a table, coffee with friends, making space for people to interrupt your space, is revolutionary. This vulnerability is where we are healed and where we find the village that cheers us on.

What can we do to fight for relationships?

Lean into Jesus for that extra dose of bravery and say yes to joining that small group, moms playdate meet-up, or book club. Open up your own space, regardless of how small and messy it may be. Word of advice: people love it when you have a normal, small, messy home. It makes everyone else feel comfortable. I'm currently going against my natural inclination to withdraw, and

4   American Psychiatric Association, "New APA poll reveals one in three Americans feels lonely," 2024.

I'm hosting a bi-weekly small group at our church. My capacity is that I can host, not cook, not clean, and my kids will not be tamed. I told everyone in our welcome email, "We are as we are, so please come as you are!" The feedback from this vibe in our home has been our biggest strength in discipleship. Sometimes, just offering what you have, where you are, is enough to foster a great community.

On this journey of saying yes, the people you surround yourself with will be your mission running buddies, handing you the Gatorade when you need it, encouraging you to keep the pace, and cheering louder than the doubts and fears. We need one another to do the thing we have been called to do. The relationships we look up to, the ones we walk side by side with, and the ones we reach back and encourage onward are all precious and beautiful expressions of God's best for us. You are not made to be an island, to do it all, be it all, and conquer it all on your own. May we be women who go against the flow and advocate for connection in its truest and purest form in our communities. May we worship wholly the triune God and seek our place in the body of Christ.

We are our absolute best when we are together. As women we know how to gather, feed, nourish, and grow together. When we say yes to this path of togetherness we are doing a great spiritual work. Oh, how we need one another to do the things God has called us to do, to bear the burden with one another through it all.

It's time to rally.

CHAPTER SIXTEEN

God of Resources

I love road trips. Our family just recently made the drive from Los Angeles to Tulsa, Oklahoma, for a summer visit. Twenty-seven hours… bless. I spent many days preparing for that drive. Our plan was to divide the trip into two parts, eleven hours to Albuquerque and another fourteen hours to Tulsa. After a few weeks in Tulsa we would be heading north to Minnesota to camp with the Norell side of the family. The girls were psyched to visit their grandparents for the summer, but they were hesitant about the drive itself. They knew the destination was worth the travel but they were heavily counting on me to provide what we needed to get there in one piece and with all our wits about us.

I packed snacks and three backpacks full of coloring paper, markers, and bracelet-making kits. Water bottles were filled, the car was cleaned, and I had a course mapped out. Like I said, I planned to make a rest stop in Albuquerque, New Mexico, so we could sleep, shower, and stretch our legs before making the second half of the trek. And before arriving in Albuquerque, I had called in and ordered food so it would be ready when we arrived because I knew the kids would be hungry. I packed a separate bag with "hotel clothes" and small toiletries. I did all I could within my power to provide what they would need on the journey.

Our road trip was a blast. My tailbone took a hit, but ultimately we were a car full of joy and adventure and Chick-fil-A sauce packets. The time and attention we took as parents to ensure a successful trip gave the kids confidence in future road trips and travels.

As we drove down a long road in the middle-of-nowhere Utah, I looked out at miles of farmland all around me. A small chopper swept low and high watering the ground just ahead of us, and God touched my heart: "Just like you take care of them, I take care of you."

Did you know God has intentionally planned and mapped out a course for the most fulfilled life you are capable of living? God sees us on our journey and He prepares the way. He is called Jireh, God our provider. God reveals Himself as provider in many ways, but today we are going to focus on two.

God provides a way *through* when we don't see a way.

God provides all *resources* for the journey He has set before us.

Setbacks to Set Ups

In the last chapter I shared about the moment the promise we felt in our heart about moving to Los Angeles was taken down from the metaphorical shelf and became our next step of obedience. We spent the next couple months closing out our time in Amsterdam and packing what we could into four suitcases, and we headed out as a family, our newest member only three months old.

Our hands were open; we were ready to pick up and move to Los Angeles the moment the pieces fell into place. But nothing was happening. Our circumstances and our promise were not lining up. In the natural, we were lacking the resources and provision to make the move, but in the spiritual we were believing and holding onto the promise of God. In our own strength this was not possible; we needed Jireh, the God who provides the job, the right school district, relationships, and the right home. In case, dear readers, you are unaware of the real estate market in Los Angeles, the cost of renting a tiny box to live in is astronomical. It had to be God who did it. Our choice of saying yes to God meant saying yes to His provision.

No one could have seen what came next.

Just writing about it gives me PTSD. COVID-19. Full stop. Y'all, I can't even. What an actual real-life mess that was. It took us all by surprise and without a doubt changed our lives forever. No one came out of the COVID-19 fog unscathed. Just as we were on the cusp of COVID-19 flipping our world upside down, I was at my friend's house, watching *The Bachelor* and eating macaroons on her couch.

"Have you heard of the coronavirus? Do you think it could come all the way over here to our small town in Oklahoma?" she said, reaching for a blanket.

"To Tulsa, Oklahoma? Nah. No way," I said in complete confidence. Naivety is bliss, people.

Not more than two weeks later while I was working the Mother's Day Out program at our church, everyone was chatting about this virus that may or may not be heading our way. It was all so confusing and at that point it was a bunch of hearsay. At the end of the day, my boss nonchalantly got a head count of everyone who was still willing to come into work the following Monday. I said yes; most of us said yes. But none of us came back to work. By the next week I no longer had a job. I was now a full-time homeschool mom and my husband was working 9-5 from our bedroom. Overnight we were forced to find a new way of living, one that involved hoarding food, not leaving the house, and micromanaging our health. It was scary and weird and the only prayer I could pray was "thy kingdom come" morning and night.

The virus felt so big and so destructive, and it was beginning to feel like it would destroy everything in its wake. Remember when the "un-shutdown-ables" started shutting down? Events like the NBA, Sunday morning church gatherings, and the Justin Bieber tour. It was wild.

Watching couples who had spent months planning their weddings say I do without friends or family with them and seeing friends of mine and other women in labor without their spouse to stand by their side in the delivery room was heartbreaking. Countless people lost their lives, suffered the loss of a friend or family member to the virus, and financial loss hit hard. It felt like we were in the middle of a *Black Mirror* episode and I wanted out.

I couldn't help but be disappointed on a micro level about what this meant for our moving plans. We never saw this coming. It all just crashed down around us. If we thought it was going to be hard to move before, it would be impossible now.

I began to do subpar on my "waiting well" skills. I was doing a lot of things well, but waiting was not one of them. I was stressing out well, not sleeping well, overthinking well, and above all else drinking too much coffee well. I had no control over the outcome and that scared me.

It was in the middle of all these doubts and fears that I received a text from a friend that said, "Lex, I just really felt like I should text you and share something with you. What seems like a setback in our eyes, God can turn into a set up."

It was like a light bulb went on in a dark hallway. Suddenly I remembered that God is God and there *ain't no thang* that can come against His will and His plans for us. It was a "but, God" moment. Did we know how or when God was going to make a way? Nope. But by placing God's character and authority over our own perspective and circumstances we ditched the fear and gained hope.

What might look like a setback in your journey toward your calling might actually be the set-up for God to be glorified. If we can simply change our perspective when we face a block in the road, we will have eyes to see the tremendous redemption God works on our behalf. The path might look different and rockier than we hoped or expected, but it's through that rough terrain that we experience the character of God most intimately. Instead of responding with utter despair and hopelessness, we can look at our setbacks as an opportunity for God to make Himself known to us, a moment that will serve as a testament of His goodness in the future.

Managing Expectations

Scripture tells us that God is not restricted by time, plot twists, or even pandemics. In fact, God says that His plans for us cannot be thwarted (Job 42:2). I want you to hear today that no matter what you are facing in your life right now, there is nothing, absolutely nothing, that can come between you and God's purposes for your life.

I have a verse for us to keep in our back pocket for a rainy day. Jeremiah 32:27 says, "I am the Lord, the God of all mankind. Is anything too hard for Me?" He is the Lord of all mankind, all the earth, over all circumstances. Nothing is above Him, nothing can defeat Him. His purposes will be victorious in your life. His kingdom will come. There is nothing that is too big, scary, or strong that can overcome God's plans. Yes and amen, that is gospel goodness for us today.

Remember the God who gave Moses the power to part the Red Sea? The God who delivered Daniel from the lions, who opened every door for Esther to set her people free, the God who provided Abraham the land He promised? What about the God who provided a Savior through a young Nazarene woman? The God who delivered us from our sin? And do you remember the God who delivered Joseph from slavery, the God who poured down manna from heaven and turned water into wine? This is the God who provides for you and makes a way for you. The same God then, today, and always.

Instead of being surprised by the challenges that come, expect them. And in the same breath, expect God's ability to make a way where we don't see a way, to set you up when all seems to be lost, where every turn feels like a dead end. God uses these moments in our lives to show us who He is and to use our testimony for others.

Along with every Bible character we read about, each of us are, in real time, experiencing the provision of God intimately in our own circumstances. You have not been excused from God's provision. You, my friend, did not single-handedly annoy God enough to have Him forget about you. He is just as deeply concerned, involved, and invested in your life as He was with Abraham, Moses, Daniel, Mary, and all the others. It is a lie of the enemy to believe that you flew under His radar, that you were somehow forgotten and unimportant.

Your story of trusting God as the provider and waymaker of your life is unfolding day by day. Saying yes to God means also saying yes to believing He will part the seas that stand between you and your promise. Saying yes means choosing to declare that He will supply you with all you need in every way as you walk in obedience toward His will.

We were in Tulsa for almost three years before we moved to Los Angeles. We worked hard, made lots of mistakes, and soon enough Josh was able to quit his full-time job and work solely for a business we'd built. In April of 2022, three years longer than we'd expected to be living in Tulsa but with a growing business in our hands, we made a scouting trip to Los Angeles. Three things were in our way to move: housing we could afford, a sustainable job, and a good school for the kids.

With the business we started and nurtured that year, the question of where we will work was taken care of. Not only did God provide us with a job, He gave us a job that allowed Josh to work remotely. While we had been praying for God to open doors for him to transfer at his previous job, God had something so much better for us and completely out of our framework of what we thought was possible. "Jehovah sneaky," right?

We flew into Los Angeles for a five-day scouting trip, to put feet on the ground as a way to be active and not passive. We had made a few scouting trips in the past and it was always such a strange thing for us. We would show up, look around, pray and wait and see if anything happened, if an area of the city "clicked." Up to this point nothing had happened, but we knew we had to continue to be open and ready.

I only had two agendas for this trip. One, check out this tiny town called South Pasadena, not to be mistaken for its neighbor, Pasadena, that I had found on a random Google search under, "family friendly areas to live in LA." I scheduled five tours of apartments I had found in that area and I had little hope they would even be available when we arrived. What I had read about South Pasadena was how wonderful the community and schools were. It was ranked up there as one of the top school districts in the entire state but was so small it was very hard to actually live within the zip code.

I jokingly asked Josh on the flight over, "Are you mentally and emotionally prepared to sign a lease this week?" He replied, "That would be insane if that happened. Let's not get ahead of ourselves." Fair.

Upon arrival I immediately got a call that two of the five apartments we were scheduled to view had been leased out. Of course they had. Shortly after that the other two called to say they had been leased out as well. Only one apartment remained. Even if we did find an apartment we could afford and that was available there was no way they were going to hold it for us for two to three months so we could go back to Tulsa, pack all our things, get renters, and then move. I wanted to be hopeful, but the odds were stacked against us.

It felt hopeless, but we knew God had called us there. I was starting to really wonder if we were crazy people for doing this. I'm sure everyone we knew thought we were irresponsible and also crazy just for moving to the West Coast, to the place so many people were moving away from due to the cost of living and political climate. We needed a miracle. This was not going to just happen—it had to be God opening a door.

We had one apartment left to see. It was located just inside the South Pasadena school district and the listing mentioned all the amenities we were hoping for. The apartment manager showed us the unit and we fell in love with it. I was careful not to get too excited because, again, it could be gone before the end of the day, and I knew they had other showings lined up. We paced around the apartment and imagined making it a home.

As we were leaving the apartment manager said, "So I would love for you guys to pick up an application on your way out. We do have other showings today so if you're interested you will need to get on that as quickly as you can because we have a first-come, first-serve policy. Secondly, I have some bad news. Unfortunately, this apartment is about to undergo a full remodel. We are replacing the floors, entire kitchen, and bathroom and repainting, so it will not be available to move into until three months from now."

My jaw almost hit the ground.

"Are you saying that if we are approved for this unit we wouldn't be able to move in for three months, and it's going to be completely remodeled?" I needed to be sure I heard him right.

"Yeah, that's right. It's been hard for us to lease it because everyone has needed something immediately, which is understandable," he said, looking at us half expecting that we would also be those people.

We grabbed the application and when we walked outside we just looked at each other. It was clear as day God had already been preparing this home for us. And just like that, our questions of where we would live and if we could find a good school district were resolved. We went to the park just down the street and sat on a bench to take it all in. We watched kids playing at the park, couples walking their dogs, and heard the wild parrots in the trees, and it felt like we were home.

We were approved for the apartment and had three months to pack and prepare to move. We couldn't believe how it all happened. How God had provided every single thing we needed and had prepared every step along the way. None of it looked the way we expected it would. Not one thing. It was so much richer and better than what we could have imagined for our family. Today, I'm living in the promise that God gave us eight years ago. To think if I had forced my timing or if God had answered the prayers I prayed the way I prayed them, our life would be way less fruitful.

God provides all the resources necessary for us to do the work.

God provides a way when we don't see a way.

In Scripture we read about the storehouse of God. He holds an abundance of supplies at the ready for us. In Job 38:22-23, it says that God has a storehouse of snow and hail for times of war. In Malachi 3:10, God says He holds a storehouse of financial provision for His people. God is not limited in His capacity of strategy and resources. It says He supplies every need necessary for us to achieve the work He has set before us. Translation: that means that what He has called you to already comes with the relationships, the financial provision, and everything down to the details of supplies, location, and daily provision.

God is serious about making a way for you. He means it when He says He will provide all you need to do the work He has given you, and He made the ultimate sacrifice of providing you with everlasting life. Again, our God is a serious provider. He will not fail you. This is who God is; it is in His nature. Take that in for a moment. You are not responsible for creating the supernatural provision needed to walk in obedience. God has already dreamed and planned how He will provide for you, the creative and beautiful ways He is going to break in and provide the tools you need to build His kingdom. He is waiting for your obedience and your faith for your invitation for Him to break in.

We have been so trained to believe that we have to wish upon a star and impress important people and pave our own paths to get anywhere. This is not true. We have only to surrender, obey, and put our faith in God. It is not our ability, connections, status, or wealth that is going to secure our dreams. If it is God's will it will be through God's provision, God's resources, and God's way.

This realization should cause massive relief in us. When we are seeking God's plan and purpose for our lives and choosing the obedience path of following Jesus, His daily portion will fill us, and our God-dreams will grow by the resources He has given us.

When you think about the God-dream you have in your heart, what are the big hindrances you see? Maybe its finances, proximity, housing, a job, or a number of other things. Out of all the voices out there that make you doubt God's provision, and on top of that, the doubts that come with what you see with your natural eyes, let me point you back to the promises of God over your life.

When He sets you on a path, He isn't going to leave you stranded, unprepared, and out to dry. No, He is going to provide you with all the things that will be required for you on the journey. He is a good Father, prepared, thoughtful, protective, and attentive. In the same way we pack the snacks, air up the car tires, and prep meals and rest stops, God is going to do the same for you on the journey He is taking you on.

God has already prepared every resource necessary for you to accomplish the calling He has given you. He holds every resource you will need to be successful on the path He has put you on. There is not one thing, big or small, that God has not already thought of. Not only that, but the dream you have in your heart is still limited by your own capacity. What you believe the fruition of that dream will look like is still not as fruitful and wonderful as the outcome that God has planned. We serve a God who supplies all we need in His perfect timing. This means that we can take a chill pill and not worry and fret over the unexpected barriers we face or the missing pieces we don't have. God has already overcome all obstacles and He is holding every resource we need along the way.

Philippians 4:19 says, "And my God shall supply all your needs according to the riches of His glory by Christ Jesus" (KJV). Saying yes to God in obedience to His way and path opens up the door for His provision and glory in our journey. And saying yes to believing in the good news of Jesus leads us into God's provision of forgiveness of our sins and communion with Him for eternity.

Our God is a provider through and through. You can build a house on this truth.

CHAPTER SEVENTEEN

One Simple, Brave Yes at a Time

If I could, I would pause time and sit with as many of you as possible just to hear you gush over the goodness of God and the dreams He has placed inside you. I love this stuff of life. I want to know everything, all the crazy, audacious dreams you have, the kind where you find yourself thinking, "God, you want me to do what now?" I wish we could meet up over a latte and unashamedly share the callings and passions God is urging us toward. I may be biased, but God really dishes out the best dreams for women, in my humble opinion. He sees us and all the hats we wear, and He reminds us that we are not simply ordinary gals but generation-changing, disciple-making, revival-carrying women. He chose women to proclaim to the world *first* that He had risen from the dead. He chose a young, simple woman to bring the actual Son of God into the world. *Talk about carrying purpose in utero!* And He is still choosing women, young and old, to proclaim His gospel and birth, dreams, solutions, and strategies into our world today.

You might still be saying, "Yeah, but why me?"

To which I say, *Why not you?*

This is your final invitation from me to join the club. The club is called, "women who are saying yes to the God-dream in their hearts and want to do it faithfully and sustainably for the rest of their livelong days" club. It is full of ordinary women who said yes to a powerful, able, extraordinary, and holy God. It's by far the best club in the history of ever. We are all seen and needed here. You don't have to strive and fight for a seat at the table because one has already been reserved just for you. We are a bunch of women who believe our surrender and obedience through love and grace has been and will continue to be the driving force of change in our homes, communities, and the world.

The best part? We don't carry the weight of it all anymore. We feel all the feels and have our struggles but we know God can take our simple but brave obedience and powerfully impact others. We understand God has a better way for us to dream, and we are choosing to take that path. He provides grace and all the necessities for us to do the work He has destined for us, and we do that work together, not against each other. It's a sisterhood in the truest sense of the word.

And, oh my stars, the dreams, you guys. Some of us are saying yes to things like foster care, going back to school after a decade away, opening a flower shop, teaching ballet classes, moving to a new city, writing the book, being a stay-at-home mom, taking the job opportunity, and all sorts of big stuff. The horizon is bright and big and magnificent, and we are better together.

Perfection is Not the Goal

Imagine with me if we all said yes to Jesus and yes to the path He has for us, what a picture that would be? If we all just said yes to the next right step of obedience, abiding and seeking communion with God as our only aim. Can you imagine the fruit and blessing and hope that would overflow from our one wild and glorious life? The generations to come would surely be blessed. If I say yes, and you say yes, and the gals down the street in a Bible study group say yes, I can't think of a better path forward for us all.

But let me remind you, saying yes to the thing you feel called to do is going to come with a side of you making a dumpster fire of a mess sometimes. That's OK! Messes are expected, failing is expected, losing our way and finding it again is all a part of the journey sometimes. You know what else we might do… self-loathe, become complacent, quit stuff real fast because we don't see the results fast enough, and a bunch of other things.

The goal here isn't perfection. This notion that practice makes perfect is a total farce. Diddly squat makes perfection, but practice does make us better. Going after your God-given dreams involves one path, God's path. Good news is that God can do incredible work with our messy obedience and surrender.

Following our yes to God isn't a situation like New Year's Day when you make a promise to start that low-carb diet and by noon January 1 you've got your arms deep into a bag of cheese puffs because kids and life and turns out you need carbs. This is not a pass or fail test. We are going to fail, and make wrong turns, and decide we know better sometimes. When this happens and you start feeling big feelings about it, just breathe and course correct. Take a nap, have a snack (it's biblical), and get back to the good work. We serve a God who is for us, who wants us to live right now in His promises. He is there in His love to pick us up, lace up our shoes, and direct our eyes back to Him.

Besides *life* happening and threatening to knock you off your path, we have a real enemy who comes to steal, kill, and destroy the plans and purposes for your life. Just read about it in John 10:10. The enemy wants to throw condemnation, worry, fear, and all sorts of lies at you to cause you to withhold your yes to Jesus. Condemnation has one fierce goal, and that's to bring you into a cycle of shame, hoping you just give up altogether. The enemy is banking on you not fully knowing the reality of God's power and grace in your life, the truth that God is mighty in our weakness. Because when we know this to be true, we understand our job is one simple but brave yes at a time, and God's got the rest.

Of all the ways our path can become challenging, let us not forget the power of grace. We need the grace of God and we will need to extend grace to ourselves. We've all heard the saying, "If you wouldn't say it to your friend, don't say it to yourself" and I think this applies here as well. You wouldn't tell a mother who is struggling to survive an awful day and thinks she's doing a terrible job that she is doomed. If you wouldn't tell a friend they should just give up, that God isn't going to provide, and He probably forgot about her, then why are you telling yourself that story? We need people to speak the truth to us, but that also starts with us reminding our spirit who our God is as well.

Be gentle with yourself. Be kind. Accept the gift of grace.

There will also be a handful of days when you simply have no idea what to do. What do you do when a season is slower than anticipated? What do you do when God is saying hold your horses and reroute? I think part of the answer can be found in the tiny book of Titus in the New Testament. Paul is writing to his friend Titus who is the pastor of the church in Crete. In his letter he emphasizes three times to, "do what is good." In Titus 3:14 he says, "Our people must learn to devote themselves to doing what is good, in order to provide for urgent needs and not live unproductive lives."

There it is. When we are out here living our lives, we can't just live for the dream. The stuff in the middle and in the waiting and in the in-betweens of every season need to be filled with doing good because it's good to be productive with good things. What good things? Being a good neighbor, a good friend, showing up for the needy, being active in making your community a little better—those kinds of good things. Put your hands to good work that glorifies God and blesses others. Do good where you can, however you can, and whenever you can. I like this road map when we feel at a stand-still. When in doubt, *do good, and be obedient to the last thing God said.*

Here's what I think. I say, go for it. I say go for it with all the assurance that God is faithful and mighty and able to do a good work in and through your life. The thing you have burning in your heart, the itch to take a step toward the calling God has put on your life, is not a no-big-deal sort of thing. Even if the step is small, take that step. One small, brave step of obedience is a powerful notion. Imagine with me if each day you said yes to a small act of obedience in one direction? Imagine what that trajectory would birth.

The Intersection of Our Surrender and God's Will

Rome wasn't built in a day, my friend; we know this. And there is nothing good and glorious that is going to come from our lives without the soil of holy grit and intention. We are building our lives, one small, seemingly insignificant step at a time. But each step is vitally important to the direction we are headed. There will never be a yes to God you will regret. Not one. Every time you say yes to Jesus and yes to His path, His pace, and His purpose, you are gaining victory in your life.

My deepest hope for you is that you don't take a single moment more to begin your journey of saying yes to God and yes to the steps of obedience He is calling you toward. Today is the day to begin. Today is the day to say that quiet prayer of surrender to the Lordship of Christ. We want so badly to submit to our own way sometimes, but I promise you that abundant life is on the other side of your surrender to our Great God. He will never let you down.

And can I say again, one last time, that we need you. We need your yes, your part in this wild story God is telling in this world. Without it, we are surely missing out. I know it can be gosh darn scary, and you risk looking foolish to take God's path. This road requires being brave, and there's no shame in shaking in your boots. Courage isn't courage without being scared. I don't know if we will ever need to stop being courageous. I don't think we will arrive at a place where the path doesn't pull us into discomfort, call us further into our insecurities, and involve our constant yielding to the Holy Spirit. But would we choose to be anywhere else? I'm convinced this is where abundant life lives: at the intersection of our surrender and God's will. This is where the magic happens. This is the place where we awaken our destiny and purpose. This is where we find true and deep intimacy with God.

They never told us that even as full-grown adult women we would still have mostly zero idea what we are doing. I believed as a kid that there would be a point I would reach where I wasn't scared anymore to speak in front of people. That I would be confident in all my decisions, obtain talents and understanding I didn't have before, and finally know what I wanted to be when I grew up. Truth is, I start and finish most things a little wobbly. My path is set but I'm clunky and doing my best. I forget things and rely on Post-it notes. Just when I think I've gotten one thing down I'm smacked with something new.

Adulting is hard. Life is messy. Winging it is the usual plan. Arriving is a unicorn. This journey of life is a big ol' journey of discovery and growth, and we will be surprised at each turn. There is not one single soul on this planet who has figured it all out, arrived at perfection, or has all the answers. We are wobbly and weird and take one step back and two steps forward all the time. I want you to remember that feeling a certain way or having life look a certain way is not a determining factor to your success in life. It may always feel weird and hard and awkward as you do the things God has called you to.

Our wobbly selves is what makes our life with Jesus so beautiful. "But God chose the foolish things of the world to shame the wise; God chose the weak things of the world to shame the strong" (1 Corinthians 1:27).

Spoiler alert: we are the foolish things. Isn't that spectacular? He sees our shortcomings, our imperfections and awkward quirks. and He thinks, *I choose her.*

The closer our proximity to God the more humble, more reliant, and more aware we are of our humanness and God's greatness. It is not about becoming more put together, sure of ourselves, or confident. It is all about Jesus, our intimate relationship with Him, our obedience to His voice, and our posture of a surrendered life.

My hope for you is that you respond to Jesus with that still, small yes in your spirit. That you will follow Him and love Him with all your heart, soul, mind, and strength. I hope you make it your life's mission to abide in proximity to His Spirit, making a home in His presence. I hope you choose to surrender your own self and purpose to His path and purpose for your life, because I know that it is wilder and more beautiful than anything you could ever imagine for yourself. I pray you don't spend a single second more camping outside of God's absolute best for you. I want to see you thriving and truly living! I hope you lean into the Holy Spirit and learn to rely on Him for all things grace, power, ability, and strength.

I also pray you become a gritty, hardworking woman, full of resilience, bravery, and courage as you walk God's path for you. I pray you learn to wait well for the promises of God that are surely coming for you, and that you know in your deepest parts that God has already provided every good thing you need for the calling He has given you. I pray you will say yes to rest and learn to say no to all that prevents you from giving your best yes to God. I pray for the grace of God to wrap you up, that you would go to Him for your daily bread.

And most of all I pray for your yes to devotion to Jesus. That the roots of your life will build a strong foundation that forms a legacy for generations to come. And from that devotion, I hope you give a bold, brave, and courageous yes to the God-dream in your heart. We need your yes.

This moment is as good as any, right now where you are. What do you see? What do you hear? What do you feel? In this present moment, in the middle of your ordinary life, ask God what the next step of bold and brave obedience looks like.

And start with yes.

BIBLIOGRAPHY

1. American Psychiatric Association. "Annual mental health poll reveals increasing anxiety among U.S. adults." Accessed May 1, 2024, https://www.psychiatry.org/news-room.

2. American Psychiatric Association. "New APA poll reveals one in three Americans feels lonely." 2024. Accessed January 30, 2024, https://www.psychiatry.org/news-room.

3. Elliot, Jim, The Journals of Jim Elliot (Revell, 1978), 172.

4. "How Many Thoughts Do You Have Each Day? And Other Things to Think About," Healthline. Accessed January 29, 2025, https://www.healthline.com/health/how-many-thoughts-per-day.

ABOUT THE AUTHOR

*Lexi Norell is a mom of three lively girls, thriving in sunny Southern California. With her relatable and humorous writing style, she weaves faith effortlessly into the rhythms of everyday life. Lexi is the author of **True North: A Devotional for the Real-Life Mom,** a heartfelt companion designed to help moms navigate motherhood with grace and authenticity.*